1980

Salem,
Transcendentalism,
and Hawthorne

Other books by Alfred Rosa

Contemporary Fiction in America and England: 1900–1950 (with Paul Eschholz)

The Old Century and the New: Essays in Honor of Charles Angoff (editor)

Salem, Transcendentalism, and Hawthorne

ALFRED ROSA

Rutherford · Madison · Teaneck
Fairleigh Dickinson University Press
London: Associated University Presses

©1980 by Associated University Presses, Inc.

Associated University Presses, Inc.
Cranbury, New Jersey 08512

Associated University Presses
Magdalen House
136–148 Tooley Street
London SE1 2TT, England

Library of Congress Cataloging in Publication Data

Rosa, Alfred F
　Salem, transcendentalism, and Hawthorne.

　Bibliography: p.
　Includes index.
　1. Salem, Mass.—Intellectual life. 2. Transcendentalism (New England) 3. Hawthorne, Nathaniel, 1804–1864—Criticism and interpretation. I. Title.
F74.S1R67　　　　974.4′5　　　　77–89784
ISBN 0–8386–2159–7

CONTENTS

Acknowledgments

Anyone who has done research at the Essex Institute in Salem, Massachusetts, knows the richness of its collections and how pleasant it is to work there. I wish to express my appreciation to the staff and especially to Irene Norton and Dorothy Potter of the Institute's library and to David Little, its former director, for their innumerable courtesies and kindnesses. They always made me feel welcome and seemed to be genuinely pleased that I found their collections helpful. I would also like to thank the staffs of the libraries of the University of Massachusetts, University of Vermont, Middlebury College, Harvard University, American Antiquarian Society, Boston Athenaeum, and Fruitlands Museums for their assistance. Edwin Gittleman, whose knowledge of Jones Very and interest in matters pertaining to Salem is immense, responded graciously to several of my inquiries and offered advice. Thanks are also due to Professors Frederick W. Turner and A. W. Plumstead of the University of Massachusetts who have commented on the text and made valuable suggestions. I feel fortunate to have been directed in this study by Professor Everett Emerson of the University of Massachusetts at whose suggestion the work was begun. His considerable erudition and industry are all that a young researcher could hope for in a model. He was patient and supportive, and I am grateful to him. Finally, I owe more than I can say to my wife, Maggie, for her sustaining belief in what I was trying to do.

INTRODUCTION

The purpose of this study is to examine the influence of Transcendentalism in Salem, Massachusetts. The first three chapters are concerned with the town itself: Chapter 1 offers a view of Salem in 1830; Chapter 2 describes the impact of Transcendentalism on Salem; and Chapter 3 describes the town's reaction to the movement. The focus of Chapter 4 is narrower and considers the personal and artistic effect Transcendentalism had on Nathaniel Hawthorne, Salem's most famous literary figure.

No investigation of this nature has yet been attempted, though the need for one seems quite apparent. Further intensive and specialized examinations of the philosophic, religious, and literary aspects of the movement tell us more and more about these particular aspects and less about Transcendentalism itself, since those studies violate the syncretic nature of the movement. This study, on the other hand, seeks to encompass the movement but to limit for practical purposes the geographic area of its influence. It is hoped that by this method some conclusions concerning the Newness, as Transcendentalism was called by its disciples, can be drawn and that these conclusions will reflect the phenomenon as a whole. How much and in what ways the movement was felt and how people reacted to it are the major questions that need to be answered.

Salem, Massachusetts was chosen as the subject of this study because it is in many ways the ideal town in which to study the effects of the Transcendental movement. Concord, the real home of Transcendentalism and its leaders, is too important to be representative. Boston is too large and cosmopolitan and thus unwieldy, and Cambridge is too much of an intellectual community in which the average citizen had been overshadowed. Salem is the right size; it is typical in many ways; it is in the heart of the region most central to Transcendentalism; it is close enough to Boston, Cambridge, and Concord; and, perhaps most importantly, it is a town that has kept detailed records of its past. The population of Salem was representative in that it had its share of important artists and intellectuals as well as middle-class people.

The first chapter of this study is a brief summary of Salem's past and an overview of the town in the year 1830, the eve of the emergence of Transcendentalism in Salem. This chapter relies heavily on quantitative analysis and statistics and measures Salem's institutions, its population, commerce, libraries, newspapers, and reading habits, and tells something about its leading citizens. Since no comprehensive cultural history has yet been written of Salem in the early decades of the nineteenth century, this overview of the town should be helpful in indicating the town's complexion before Transcendentalism began to have an influence there.

The second chapter is concerned more properly with Transcendentalism in Salem. It presents a close study of Salem's lyceum, its objectives, method of operation, and its importance as a means of disseminating the new philosophy. The part played by Ralph Waldo Emerson and the Transcendentalism of his lectures, as well as a treatment of the other figures who gave lectures that embodied the Transcendental philosophy, is then discussed. Finally, this second chapter turns to a treatment of Elizabeth Palmer Peabody and Jones Very, two Salem intellectuals who were intimately involved in the Transcendental movement. An investigation of their philosophies and works serves to show the rise of the Newness within the town itself as well as its connection with forces outside Salem.

Chapter 3 describes and assesses the responses to Transcendentalism in Salem. This chapter, like the previous one, uses contemporary newspaper reviews to help determine Salem's attitudes toward the Newness. A recounting of Jones

Very's confrontations with several Salem ministers is then presented, and the social ties that linked Hawthorne, Sophia Peabody, Emerson, and Very are revealed.

Salem does not make an ideal subject for historical analysis, and the method for describing the influences on it is far from infallible, for Salem presents problems common to any town one attempts to study, in addition to those that are peculiar to itself. Any present-day attempt to determine the matrix of place, of feelings, influences, reactions, and moods in a town is difficult. The task is an especially difficult matter for a period over one hundred years removed from us and is, therefore, subject to a degree of distortion and inaccuracy from the very beginning. An investigator must be all things at once: historian, sociologist, economist, demographer, political scientist, and psychologist. The coordination of a multipronged approach of this sort is not easy. One must be aware of the great tendency to oversimplify or to reduce complexities to their lowest common denominator. In addition, there is the task of determining the weight that should be given to each area of interest in every situation. It would be difficult enough to coordinate all of these interests if a town were to remain unchanged over a period of years, but towns never remain static and shaping influences must be separated from normal growth. These are only some of the questions that arise, however, and they are not unique to Salem. Although the investigative methodology presents its own problems, it is probably still the best way of developing a comprehensive view of a town.

Salem also had problems of a more specialized nature. Changes in the town profoundly altered its self-image. After the collapse of its important sea trade, Salem attempted to make a name for itself as an industrial power. This attempt at revitalization failed and the town never really regained its former economic strength. Such a shift in economic emphasis had inevitable ramifications on the town's social and cultural makeup. Salem no longer had contact with the great ports of the world and the cultural influence that those ports provided. It had then to look on its culture as a historical fact, a thing of the past essentially, rather than something that was still developing and expanding. In 1830 an event occurred that lifted Salem onto the front page of every newspaper in the country: the famous White murder case, the first criminal case in this country to receive national press coverage. It was an exciting and frightful time for Salem since the trial, although carried out under legal procedures, echoed the famous Salem witchcraft trials of the seventeenth century. Many people were under suspicion for the murder. Daniel Webster was brought in to act as a prosecuting attorney, and the final result of the trial was the execution of the murderers of Captain White. The image of Salem as a quiet, secluded New England seaport was shattered with rumors of conspiracies, financial collapses, and threats of further violence. Newspaper reports of thousands of Salemites viewing the executions of the murderers did little for the town's reputation.

Lastly, there was a great social and intellectual awakening in the form of the lecture or lyceum system that began to evolve in Salem, as it was evolving in every small town in the country. Salem's lyceum was one of the biggest and most famous and attracted almost every important lecturer to its platform. The effects of these lyceum lectures on Salemites was very great and was especially beneficial for the cause of Transcendentalism, and yet it is another one of those influences whose precise effect is finally difficult to evaluate.

Salem is also a good place to assess the influence of Transcendentalism and the reaction to it because it was the home of Nathaniel Hawthorne, whose connections to the Transcendental movement were many and involved. Hawthorne was encouraged very early in his career by his wife's sister, Elizabeth Palmer Peabody, a member of the Transcendental group, and his wife Sophia was sympathetic to the Newness and was a close friend of Ralph Waldo Emerson's. Hawthorne himself was a friend of Jones Very's, a minor Salem Transcendentalist, a mystic, and a sonneteer of considerable skill. After Hawthorne's stay at Brook Farm, the much publicized Transcendental Utopian community, he and his wife moved to Concord, the center of New England Transcendentalism. In Concord, Hawthorne came to know Emerson, Thoreau, Alcott, the younger Channing, and Margaret Fuller, leading Transcendentalists who lived there. Whether or not Hawthorne was a Transcendentalist or to what degree he accepted or rejected that philosophy has long been an area of controversy.

In an article written in 1904, Bliss Perry discussed the issue of Hawthorne's relationship to Puritanism but went on to suggest on the basis of some rather weak evidence, Hawthorne's reading and friendship with other Transcendentalists, that Hawthorne was a Transcendentalist.[1] Frank P. Stearns said in *The Life and Genius of Nathaniel Hawthorne* (1906) that Hawthorne "was emphatically an idealist, as every truly great artist must be, and Transcendentalism was the local costume which ideality wore in Hawthorne's time."[2] Stearns lightly dismisses Hawthorne's anti-Transcendentalism because "there could have been no malice in his satire, for Mrs. Hawthorne's two sisters, Mrs. Mann and Miss Peabody, were both transcendentalists."[3] Stearns also says that "the essence of Transcendentalism is the assertion of the indestructibility of spirit, that mind is more real than matter, and the unseen than the seen," and that no writer of the nineteenth century "affirms this more persistently than Hawthorne."[4] In 1918, John Erskine referred to Hawthorne as a Transcendentalist and defended Hawthorne's skepticism as revelatory of his true Transcendentalism: "He was really the questioner, the detached observer, that other Transcendentalists thought they were."[5] In 1931, Henry Seidel Canby wrote of Hawthorne that "Emerson interested him, Margaret Fuller fascinated him, Thoreau got his admiration—but Transcendentalism as such touched him not at all."[6] Austin Warren's *Nathaniel Hawthorne: Representative Selections* (1934) is interesting in this context for its "Introduction," which contains a surprisingly full treatment of Hawthorne's anti-Transcendentalism.[7] It is an overstatement but an early treatment and useful for its references.

It was not until 1941 and the publication of F. O. Matthiessen's *American Renaissance* that any one of these critics looked at all of Hawthorne's writings in an attempt to put this relationship in the proper perspective.[8] Matthiessen was the first to state that Hawthorne did have some intellectual kinship with the Transcendentalists but that he was strongly opposed to the Transcendental attitudes toward reform in particular,[9] that the problem was much more complicated than simple answers would serve and that it must be stated as such. Floyd Stovall's *American Idealism*, which followed in 1943, saw Hawthorne as adhering to some Transcendental tenets.[10] Three more recent treatments of the subject have also recognized its problematical nature. Millicent Bell's *Hawthorne's View of the Artist* (1962) correctly sees Hawthorne's anti-Transcendentalism as a part of the inherent anti-romanticism found in the romantic period in both England and America.[11] Although her hypothesis is interesting, she fails to support it with a convincing amount of specific documentation. In her *Nathaniel Hawthorne: Transcendental Symbolist* (1969), Marjorie Elder specifically refuses to discuss whether or not Hawthorne was a Transcendentalist but rather seeks to determine if he was a Transcendental symbolist; she finally concludes he was.[12] Her denial notwithstanding, Miss Elder's major point is that Hawthorne was a Transcendentalist. Finally, in "American Values and Romantic Fiction" (1977), Milton R. Stern provides a more convincing elaboration of the anti-romanticism thesis put forth by Bell.[13] In short, he suggests that all serious writers of the period were faced with the peculiar dilemma of how, on the one hand, to reach wider audiences without appearing to give into popular tastes they despised and how, on the other hand, to keep from giving themselves over to the millennialism of the Transcendentalists. [14]

Chapter 4 of this study discusses some facts of Hawthorne's early life and then moves to a more detailed and chronological analysis of his major novels and short stories: the ways he expressed his attitudes concerning the Newness in his writing as well as his relationship to Brook Farm and the Transcendentalists. Hawthorne made few public comments about Transcendentalism; it is chiefly in his fiction that one can determine his attitudes toward the movement. It is for this reason that Chapter 4 depends mainly on literary analysis and criticism for its conclusions regarding these beliefs.

Hawthorne, like Salem itself, presents some problems for a study of Transcendentalism in Salem. As Hyatt Howe Waggoner has pointed out, there are many Hawthornes. [15] There is Hawthorne the Salemite, but there is also the Hawthorne who lived and wrote in Concord. There is the vengeful Hawthorne who caused a considerable amount of animosity in Salem when he wrote "The Custom House" sketch for the preface to *The Scarlet Letter* and who, although realizing that he had created ill will, continued to have the sketch published in succeeding editions. There is also Hawthorne the writer whose father died when Hawthorne was four years old, as well as the Hawthorne who suffered an injury to his foot as a boy, which has been seen as the cause for his later isolation. There is further the recluse of sorts, the happily married but shy writer, the man of extreme sensitivity approaching at times sentimentality, and the skeptic who could more easily find faults than virtues in the people and actions that revolved around him. There is also the distant, aloof, cold, and detached Hawthorne who puts so much of himself into the figure of Miles Coverdale in *The Blithedale Romance*, the Paul Pry who peers into the lives of those around him and who, to some extent like Ethan Brand, looks for the evil that lurks in their hearts. Another Hawthorne, however, married Sophia Peabody who understood Transcendentalism, knew and felt some compassion for Jones Very, lived at Brook

Farm and in Concord, and walked and talked with Emerson, Alcott, and Thoreau. This Hawthorne, strangely enough, disliked reformers because he felt that the reformist zeal was but a projection of the reformer's own sense of inadequacy. But these are only some of the ironies and paradoxes that must be considered when dealing with a figure who above all else was an independent thinker with immense creative talent. The degree to which Hawthorne is representative of Salem is a difficult matter to determine if such a determination should even be attempted. The treatment of him, however, is finally necessary in balancing out the picture that is presented of Salem in the earlier part of this study, for no investigation of Transcendentalism in Salem can ignore the town's greatest son, whose relationship to the movement and its disciples is undeniably important.

The complexities of the method and the subject of the research as discussed thus far are formidable and they are increased, not lessened, when an evaluation of the Transcendental movement is the objective. As a philosophical and literary phenomenon, Transcendentalism avoided definition and categorization, and its force and degree of influence are not always easily detected. Quite naturally, reactions to it are often subjective, hasty, and without direction. Yet, its presence was felt in Salem; there were reactions to it and generalizations about forces, counterforces, and the attitudes of Salemites can be made and supported.

Transcendentalism embodied a number of new attitudes regarding man's relationship to the universe and the quality of the life that he leads. Emerson asked that very question: "Why should we not enjoy an original relation to the universe?"[16] and implicit in that plea is the rejection of hollow materialism and the past. This "original relation" for the Transcendentalists was to be accomplished by putting a higher priority on feeling as opposed to thinking as well as on the development of man's aesthetic faculties rather than those aimed at greater materialism and cupidity. There was a pervasive optimism in all of this and it stood in direct and outward contrast to the emphasis on sin and evil that characterized Puritan theology, an emphasis that lingered in the thinking and writings of Nathaniel Hawthorne.

Salem,
Transcendentalism,
and Hawthorne

SALEM IN 1830

FEW American cities can be as proud of their origins or take greater delight in the motivations of their founders as the city of Salem, Massachusetts. Many of the first settlers of Salem, then called Naumkeag, did not come to this country in expectation of material wealth, a better climate, natural resources, trade, or the goals that usually caused men to disrupt their lives and break their traditional ties and start anew. The first settlers of Salem crossed the Atlantic in 1626 to escape religious persecutions and to seek the free and independent life that had eluded them for so long in the Old World. The first few years in the New World were not easy and the problems Roger Conant, who settled Salem, and his people encountered made clear to them the profundity and magnitude of the project they had undertaken.

After the original Salem settlement was made by the Council of England, John Endicott was appointed governor of the plantation that until that time had been given only a grant of property without authority to establish a government. Endicott then headed the corporation called the "Governor and Company of the Massachusetts Bay in New England," which lasted for more than a half century.[1]

During Endicott's period of rule the early colonists were ever watchful that their civil and ecclesiastical rights not be violated and their agitations served to emphasize the difficulties arising from the great distance separating the ruling and colonizing bodies of the Council of England. On August 29, 1629, the Council selected John Winthrop to be the colony's governor, invested him with much more power than Endicott had enjoyed, and directed him to sail for Salem, where he arrived on July 12, 1630. The arrival of Winthrop and his subsequent choice of Charlestown, Massachusetts, as his head-quarters precluded that Salem be the capital as it seemed for a time destined to be. It was the uncommon faith and fortitude of the first planters of Salem, however, that must have made the whole venture in the New World seem possible, and those early crucial years constitute a more substantial source of greatness than any growth or governmental authority could have provided.

Salem in the 1630s encompassed what is now Beverly, Danvers, Marblehead, Topsfield, Wenham, and Lynn, Mas-sachusetts. Each of these settlements later became a separate town, leaving what we now know to be Salem. Before Salem was made a city in 1836, its importance, if somewhat less than it had been, continued to be considerable. Salem had sent Roger Williams out of its church and community, had seen Governor Endicott cut the Red Cross from the English ensign, had detestably persecuted the Quakers in Salem village, and had infamously executed nineteen "witches."

If there is any truth in the saying that history is little more than the record of disasters and calamities, there was little history being made in Salem in the period between the Revo-lution and the installation of Leverett Saltonstall as Salem's first mayor. History, however, is much more than dilemma. It is the record of the growth of a people, and Salem during the thirty-five years that followed the Revolution experienced a commercial and naval expansion that not only made it a leading port in this country but also made the name Salem a commonplace in every known port in the world.[2] The men of Salem built bigger, stronger, and faster ships than had ever before sailed the seas and by 1807 the men of Salem owned 252 vessels with a total weight of 43,570 tons. The great mer-chant Joseph Peabody owned eighty-three ships, had seven thousand seamen at his disposal, and had promoted forty-five cabin boys to the rank of captain. Another important merchant, Elias Derby, had opened the Far East to trade; when he died he left the largest fortune, $1,500,000, that at the time had been amassed in this country.[3] Sailors from this small New England town were known and respected wherever people carried on trade in the world, and the variety and quality of the goods that streamed onto its wharves and into its warehouses would stagger the imagination even today.

The period between 1815 and 1845, however, saw the decline of Salem as a leading commercial and trade center. The Embargo Act of 1807, the War of 1812, and the politics of Massachusetts Federalism had all served to slow down the momentum of Salem's trade and dampen the great profits that had been enjoyed by its people.[4] More importantly, Salem's harbor was neither very wide nor very deep, and when trade finally began to increase generally, the ports at Boston and New York were found to be more adequate physically. During the period 1815–1845 all trade dropped off and then, once again, began to climb to new heights, but Salem could not hold its position behind Boston and New York as a shipping center.[5] The decline of Salem as a shipping center did not mean that all shipping in Salem declined drastically. Salem's shipping continued to increase but not at the rate that it did in Nantucket, Barnstable, and New Bedford.

With the decline of Salem's shipping came a period of relative quiet such as the town had not enjoyed since before the Revolution. Salem's townspeople appreciated the lull, but they were never really proud of it. They were not content to sit back, even though some of them could well afford to do so, and let things take their course. They had a town to run and perhaps secretly hoped to recapture Salem's past commercial glories. They tried whale hunting and found it to be a very dangerous business; they tried manufacturing and found that it did not pay the high profits to which they were accustomed. By 1845, Salem had ceased to be a town of any real commercial importance. As the sea and sailing became less and less a part of the lives of prominent Salemites, they abandoned their homes near the wharves and warehouses and moved to the interior of the town where their fashionable homes can still be seen today.

In 1830 the population of Salem was 13,886 of which 88 people were foreigners.[6] Of the approximately 230 deaths in that year[7] the main causes were consumption, which took 50 lives; "old age," which caused the deaths of 21; lung fever, which took 20 lives; and "dropsy in the head," of which 15 died.[8] There were about 125 marriages[9] and 491 births.[10] Some of the town's leading figures were Dr. Edward A. Holyoke, a prominent physician; John Pickering, one of America's earliest and most distinguished linguists who prepared the first Greek-English dictionary; Nathaniel Hawthorne, one of America's most distinguished authors; Jones Very, poet and Greek scholar; Charles W. Upham, Whig politician, minister, and later mayor; Joseph Peabody, merchant; Elias Derby, merchant; and the Nathaniel Peabody family, which, although it had moved from Salem to Boston in 1828, was still considered to be a part of Salem.[11] Dr. Peabody, a dentist, was the father of Sophia, who was to become the wife of Nathaniel Hawthorne; Mary, who was to marry Horace Mann; and Elizabeth, who was to be an instrumental figure in the Transcendental movement. Elizabeth was engaged in a teaching venture with William Russell and had taken the whole family to Boston with her. Dr. Peabody was reluctant to leave Salem and his practice and was furthermore not sure whether Elizabeth's new undertaking would be successful. On September 10, 1830, two years after the family had officially left Salem, Dr. Peabody was still placing advertisements in the Salem *Gazette* indicating that he, at least, still felt something for the town:

> Dr. Peabody continues to visit Salem the first and third Thursday of every month—for the purpose of operating upon Teeth. His off. is at Mr. S. S. Page's corner of Essex

and Summer streets.

As a report is abroad that Dr. Peabody has raised his fees for operating upon teeth, he takes this opportunity to state that it is not true; his fees are the same as they always have been.[12]

These were the important residents of the town, some of whom were also the wealthiest, and their stature was balanced on the other end of the economic scale by the 236 poor people who were maintained solely by welfare.[13] Salem had built an almshouse in 1815, and the town had a record of paying high taxes to the commonwealth and aiding other communities, near and far, that had been the victims of various catastrophes. Salem had numerous charitable organizations to aid those, in addition to the town's poor, who were not quite so destitute.[14]

The overwhelming majority of the population of Salem was employed in providing the essential products and services by which any community exists. The number of people engaged in local trade and vending must have been about two hundred in 1830.[15] Many more people were engaged in Salem's greatest industry, shipbuilding. From 1789 to 1843, Salem built "61 ships, 4 barks, 53 brigs, 3 ketches, and 16 schooners, whose measurement was 30,559 tons."[16] During the five years preceding 1836, the town's shipwrights had manufactured nine ships of 2,495 tons total.[17] It is difficult to tell just how many men were engaged in this trade and for that matter just how many men were sailors. If a young man in the early nineteenth century did not learn one of the numerous trades, which ranged from candle making to stone masonry and which engaged only handfuls of men in Salem, he had two main options open to him. He could farm, and, if he was uncommonly industrious, he could save enough money over a number of years to buy his own farm. Or, he could go to sea where the work was very dangerous and difficult, but where he could make enough money in a few years to marry and buy a farm and live comfortably the rest of his life. This latter alternative was very popular as can be seen by the ships' records of the period, which indicate that a vast majority of the sailors were in their teens and twenties, fewer in their thirties, and practically none in their forties.[18]

The manufacture of lead, chiefly for use in making paint, was a major industry at this time and Salem produced almost 900,000 pounds of lead between 1829 and 1833.[19] Lead making in Salem was a temporary business, however, and not nearly as stable as the tanning of hides, which was done in about twenty-three Salem tan houses in 1830.[20] Rope and sail making, chaise and coach making, hat making, brewing, distilling, cigar making, and baking were the other chief industries of the town. The manufacturing of clothing was attempted in 1826 as another means of helping the lagging economy, but ceased in 1830.[21] The making of clothing had drawn criticism and was curtailed although it had not been proven to be a failure. It seems likely that Salem was losing its commercial sea trade but was not psychologically or technologically ready for an industrial way of life.[22]

There were about a dozen churches in Salem in 1830. The First Congregational Society had the Rev. Charles W. Upham as its minister; the East Church had James Flint from 1825 to 1851; Saint Peter's, an Episcopal church, had the Rev. Alexander V. Griswold from 1829 to 1834; and the Tabernacle Church had the Rev. John P. Cleveland, D.D. from 1827 to 1834. The North Church's minister was the well-known John Brazer, who served that church from 1820 until he died in 1846. Brazer delivered the Dudleian Lecture at Harvard on May 13, 1835, and received the Doctor of Divinity degree in the same year. The South Church was served by the Rev. Brown Emerson from 1805 until his death, which presumably occurred about the middle of the century. The First Baptist Church had settled Lucius Bolles in 1805, who resigned from the position in 1834. The Second Baptist Church was served by Cyrus P. Grosvenor from 1830 to 1834; the

First Universalist Church had settled Lemuel Willis in 1829 and he served that society until 1837. The only Roman Catholic Church in Salem was the pastorate of Rev. John Mahoney. The Methodist Church was served by Jesse Filmore from 1822 until 1832, and the Independent Congregational Church was served by Henry Colman from 1825 to 1831. Other small religious groups worshipped together and several black churches existed for short periods, but their histories are somewhat obscure.

The establishment of public schools in Salem in 1640 occurred at about the same time that Boston established its first schools. The historians of these events leave some doubt as to which community began its public education first.[23] By 1878, Salem had 1,200 students enrolled in its schools, but we can only conjecture at the number enrolled in 1830. Although the education of females had long been accepted, they did not usually attend school with males. The year 1830 was an important year for black students as a black girl's right to attend the girls' high school was "questioned but affirmed."[24] Although a precedent was set by the decision to allow the black girl to attend that school, a group of Salem citizens showed some displeasure at the move and in 1834 a special room was set aside for the education of black girls.[25]

Salem's intellectual interests never lagged behind its commercial successes. The townspeople were always conscious of the town's importance and sought to preserve as much of its history as possible. By 1830, Salem had about a dozen libraries with a combined holding of about 31,000 printed volumes with additional manuscripts and historical documents.[26] The character of Salem's culture is clearly indicated by its libraries:

1. The Library of Arts and Sciences, founded 1802.
2. The Fourth Social Library, founded 1806.
3. Essex South District Medical Library, founded 1805 (900 volumes).

4. The Salem Evangelical Library, founded 1818 (500 volumes, housed in Dr. B. Emerson's house).
5. The Salem Charitable Mechanic Association, founded 1817 (2,400 volumes).
6. The Salem Military Library, founded 1818.
7. The East India Marine Museum, founded 1799 (250 printed volumes as well as manuscripts and curiosities).
8. Essex Historical Society, founded 1821 (1,400 volumes, portraits, and other items of historical interest).
9. Salem Athenaeum, incorporated March 12, 1810 (about 11,000 volumes; comprised of what were previously the holdings of smaller libraries).
10. Essex Bar Library, founding date unknown (600 volumes).
11. Essex County Natural History Society, not officially founded until 1831 (650 volumes).
12. Sabbath and public school libraries, founding dates unknown (11,000 volumes).

The holdings in the town's libraries exhibit a wide range of interests and professional concerns. Additional sources of knowledge and reading enjoyment were provided by the reading rooms, an institution that remains only vestigially today. These were often opened to satisfy particular needs and closed when those needs were fulfilled. The reading rooms organized for general purposes and readers were The Mechanic (1827) and Buffum's (1831); for the dissemination of political news and information, The Democratic (1827) and The National Republican (1832); and for city news, The Commercial (1825).[27] Two circulating libraries, "purveyors of 'light reading,'" one maintained by John M. Ives and the other by Mrs. Hannah Harris in 1830, together contained about four thousand volumes.[28] Many Salemites also maintained personal libraries, which they used to educate themselves and to keep abreast of the progress of knowledge and world events.

The history of the early years of printing in Salem is not

very significant. Boston had established a public press in 1637, and Cambridge followed with its press in 1639. Although Salem was the third town in Massachusetts to print its own writings, it did not enjoy that privilege until 1768, more than a century and a quarter after Boston. There were several reasons for the delay. The clergy in Salem held tight rein on all printing, not just religious materials, and freedom of the press was not truly gained until the Revolution. Salem, of course, recognized the need for a press very early; and the Cambridge press, although not very convenient, did serve Salem's purposes. The fact that Salem was without its own printing facilities does not mean that its citizens were intellectually dormant.[29] All kinds of materials, including sermons, tracts, addresses, and church quarrels were written, printed, and distributed.

In 1830 the chief printers in Salem were Caleb Foote, Warwick Palfrey, and William and Stephen Ives. There were of course other printers including John Archer, James R. Buffum, John D. Cushing, and the firm of Whipple and Lawrence, but the first mentioned were the leaders in the industry.[30] Printing was not as specialized as it is now; a newspaper was the mainstay of a printer's livelihood; book publishing, selling, and editing were all part of the same business but these activities were always incidental and peripheral. Foote and William Brown, Jr., put out the Salem *Gazette* and Palfrey was the editor of the *Essex Register*. William and Stephen Ives published the *Observer*, later named the *Salem Observer*. Charles A. Andrew edited the *Salem Courier*, which ceased publication only a few months prior to 1830, and William and Stephen Ives published the *Hive*, a juvenile weekly, which published its final issue in September 1830, a year after it had begun publication. Another publication, the *Ladies' Miscellany*, published from January 1829 to January 1830, was issued from the office of the *Register* and was undoubtedly put out by Mr. Palfrey.[31]

Four bookstores of any significance were operating in Salem in 1830. These were run by John D. Wilson, Henry

Whipple, John M. Ives, and John W. Archer. It seems clear from the records of its newspaper, magazine, and book publications that Salem did not suffer from its late start in establishing its own printing offices. It should also be noted that the preceding only describes what was done in Salem itself and does not take into account the books, newspapers, and magazines that were brought into Salem by retailers, the mails, or private persons. By 1830 the reading of Salem's more than 13,500 people seems to have been taken care of quite adequately.

Reading, however great a source of enjoyment, was only one among many forms of diversion for Salemites. In January 1828, the Mechanic Association began to have a course of lectures that were to be continued annually.[32] Lectures were not very commonly given in Salem or elsewhere at this time although Joseph Felt records that lectures on botany, chemistry, mnemonics, astronomy, the structure of the earth, and various other topics were given in Salem between 1812 and 1830.[33] There were also recitations from the works of English and American authors and dramatic readings by men and women who traveled in circuits, advertised their performances, and charged admissions.

In 1829 and 1830, however, a totally new spirit in lecturing broke forth with the beginning of the American lyceum movement.[34] This movement, discussed in more detail in Chapter 2, added an important dimension to the lives of the common people especially and was a phenomenon that was as popular as it was influential and significant. Its importance to Salem is overshadowed only by its effect on the country as a whole.

Visits to the various museums and libraries—exhibiting strange and exotic stuffed birds and animals, rare plants, pottery, jewelry, art, weapons, and artifacts of every conceivable kind, not only from all the distant ports that Salem's seamen had visited but also from Salem's own history—were another form of amusement. In the early part of the nineteenth century Indians were so uncommon in Salem that they constituted a curiosity in themselves, and the Salemites could learn something of the early inhabitants of Salem whenever an Indian returned to the area.[35]

Hawthorne thought the East India Marine Society Museum worthy enough to take his then famous former Bowdoin classmate, Franklin Pierce, and his friend Samuel Dinsmore there when they visited him in Salem in the mid-1830s.[36] The Salem East India Society had as one of its original intentions the aid and support of children who had been orphaned by the death of seamen, particularly shipmasters. As Hawthorne himself was one of the objects of the society's good works, he enjoyed membership, which was otherwise limited to captains, and felt justifiably proud of the society and his membership in it.

In 1828, Charles Osgood, a young portrait painter, returned to Salem, his native town, and set up his studio.[37] In 1840 he painted the portrait of the young Salem writer Nathaniel Hawthorne, a commission that would perhaps bring Osgood his greatest fame.[38] Joseph True, a sculptor, was the only other professional artist in the town at the time, although many people drew, painted, and made silhouettes, a popular nineteenth-century artistic endeavor.

Salem's wealthiest citizens had enjoyed the services of its great Federalist architect Samuel McIntire (1757–1811)[39] for some years prior to 1830, and his works were visible everywhere one turned in the town. He not only had designed the stately houses of many of the wealthy Salemites but he also had planned their public buildings, the Court House, assembly halls, and the South Meeting House. McIntire's work and influence and the simultaneous withdrawal of Salem's wealthy from Derby Street and the waterfront helped to make Essex Street, Washington Square, and especially Chestnut Street, "the finest street architecturally in New England,"[40] a very beautiful area.

In June 1825, a Mozart Association was begun and on March 9, 1826, it sponsored its introductory concert in the First Church.[41] The association's trustees were Leverett Saltonstall,

Horatio Perry, Henry K. Oliver, William Kimball, Seth Low, Jacob Hood, Henry Hubon, Theodore Eames, and Edwin Jocelyn. [42] The town had received numerous musical performers and had given many musicales throughout its history; the formation of a Mozart Association, one of the first of its kind in this country, impresses us much more today perhaps than it impressed the people of Salem at that time.

Dramatic presentations were never really popular in Salem or in Boston, or at least popular demand for such performances was sufficiently suppressed by the authorities that the presentations of plays were infrequent. Actors, more so than plays, were still looked upon as immoral, and puritanical attitudes held sway. On February 4, 1828, however, a building on Crombie Street was opened for the presentation of plays, but as Felt says: "This was far from meeting the general wish of the inhabitants." [43] After a trial period that lasted four years, the owners of the theater decided that it was unprofitable and closed it. Felt concludes his statement on theatrical performances with the following moralistic comment that gives us a further insight into the nature of the prejudices against the theater: "Our citizens have found it a much more profitable mode of spending their time and money, to hear lectures on interesting and useful subjects, than to congregate for the purpose of listening to actors." [44]

. Less intellectual, but much more spectacular, was the continual procession of circus and vaudeville types that visited Salem between 1825 and 1835. [45] These included ventriloquists, magicians, acrobats, and "invisible" men and women who were often accompanied by animals and exhibits featuring wax images, works of art, and human birth defects. Felt states amusingly that, although he will not discuss the plausibility of such a thing, he does wish to report that a mermaid was exhibited in Salem on July 5, 1824. [46] Unabashedly, however, he reports for 1835: "A collection of animals visits us. In this was the unicorn." [47]

Various other casual pastimes could be enjoyed by the Salemite of 1830. One could walk to the top of Gallows Hill, as Hawthorne was accustomed to doing, and look out to the sea and perhaps be the first to spot an incoming ship.[48] One could also walk to the water's edge and watch the building, outfitting, or unloading of a ship, or one could sail out into the harbor, drop anchor at some shore point, and enjoy a picnic lunch, this being perhaps the most frequent and enjoyable pastime for the people of Salem.

There was little that was visibly unusual about Salem's social structure in 1830. Most people were hard-working, middle-class citizens; there were few poor and still fewer very rich. Salem's wealthy enjoyed themselves as befitted their genteel station; the middle-class citizens worked hard and partook of what pleasures their work allowed; and the poor were understandably preoccupied with their subsistence. On the morning of April 7, 1830, however, Salem's tranquility was suddenly shattered. The body of eighty-three-year-old Captain Joseph White was found in his bed; he had been viciously murdered.[49] The murder shocked the country, and it was the first event of its kind to achieve national press coverage. Preliminary investigations and the trial that followed revealed that beneath Salem's quiet façade there existed an intriguing and mysterious subculture that might have otherwise gone unrecorded: "the bankruptcy of the merchants, the vice in connection with emerging industry, the depravity that reached into the families of men whose fleets, a generation before, had circled the earth."[50] Tales of vice and evil characters were on the lips of everyone in the town; everyone was suspect, and an atmosphere not unlike that of the witch trials prevailed.

George and Richard Crowninshield and Joseph and John Francis Knapp were eventually arrested for the murder. Richard Crowninshield later committed suicide in his cell. Daniel Webster was appointed as a special prosecutor and eighty witnesses, many of them leading citizens of Salem, were called to testify at the trial.[51] The Knapps were eventually

hanged for the murder of White because they had hired
Richard Crowninshield to murder the old man for the in-
heritance they had hoped to receive. Joseph Knapp was hanged
on September 28 and John Francis Knapp met a similar end
before a crowd of four thousand Salemites on the last day
of the year.[52] There is no evidence that George Crowninshield
was ever convicted.

Hawthorne left Salem some time before John Francis Knapp
was executed and it is thought that his decision to leave might
have had something to do with the trial. Everyone was under
suspicion and Hawthorne may have realized the precariousness
of his position. As a writer he was not gainfully employed,
was something of a recluse, and might have feared being
implicated in the murder. It is possible that the atmosphere
created by this trial was a part of Hawthorne's own "history,"
his psychic history, if you will, that had come to haunt him
and drive him from Salem.[53] Perhaps, the very specter of
his great-great-great-grandfather, one of the judges at the
witchcraft trials, had risen before him again and frightened
the young writer into fleeing Salem.

In 1830 the town of Salem had a very strong sense of its
own identity, history, and importance. Salem was two cen-
turies old in 1830, and it had sought to preserve its history
not only in its museums and libraries but also in the minds
of its citizens. Samuel McIntire's stately architecture reminded
Salemites in 1830, as it reminds us today, of the image of
solidarity, stateliness, and simplicity that the town's leading
citizens hoped to put forth to the world.

The sea opened Salem to influences from all over the world
and linked it to many parts of this country by the goods that
left and entered Salem's ports. Trade made the town wealthy,
provided jobs, and, above all, maintained a progressive spirit
that served to balance the town's strong sense of the past.

Salem's most famous citizens, Hawthorne, Very, Upham,
Saltonstall, Peabody, Pickering, Brazer, Derby, and Holyoke,
were also famous citizens of the United States. Cultural op-

portunities were readily available, schools were progressive, and many of Salem's young men went off to Harvard for their education but then returned to the town. Salem kept abreast, if not actually in the vanguard, of contemporary developments and thought in American life.

TRANSCENDENTALISM IN SALEM

T HE Salem Lyceum must be closely examined for a study of Transcendentalism in Salem. The Salem Lyceum was the chief medium for the expression of Transcendental ideas, and it was there that the Transcendentalists had their greatest and most immediate impact on the people of Salem, and where exciting speakers breathed life into the various aspects of the new philosophy. Concord had, as Carl Bode says, a more intellectual lyceum, but it was Salem that perhaps best exhibited in a general way all of the admirable purposes of the lyceum movement.[1] Some of the more important of these purposes were (1) to improve conversation in general by having lecturers present intellectually sound but, above all, useful information for the betterment of the whole community; (2) to direct community amusements and entertainments; (3) to save expenses by providing activities for a great number of people so that a year's entertainment could be had for between fifty cents and two dollars; (4) to rejuvenate neglected libraries and call into greater use already active libraries; (5) to provide a seminary for teachers and thus raise the character of the teacher in general; (6) to improve the character of schools; (7) to compile town histories, draw maps, and sponsor agricultural and geological surveys; and (8) to assume local responsibility for statewide industrial and agricultural projects.[2]

The beginnings of the Salem Lyceum go back to a meeting held in Topsfield in December 1829 to plan the formation of a county lyceum. It was decided at that time that such a county lyceum should be an outgrowth of small, local lyceums, and Salem was chosen as a logical town for such an experiment. A short time later Charles Upham, a Salemite, sent out a circular letter describing the actions and resolutions of the group and explaining what the Salem Lyceum had already established as a constitution.[3] Upham further explained that the lyceum would not have to look too far for lecturers since many prominent local citizens could often be called upon to lecture. He then made an interesting connection between the decline of business (and here it seems obvious that Salem was his point of reference) and the beginning of the lyceum system:

> The decline of commerce, and the stagnation of mercantile business, having thrown out of employment a large number of inhabitants of our seaboard town, who, if they could be engaged in the acquisition and communication of knowledge, would be provided, at the same time, with a resource most agreeable to their own feelings, and with the means of being useful to others. If their leisure hours were thus occupied, they would be laying up stores of information which would be highly beneficial to them in whatever pursuits they might afterwards be engaged.[4]

Here, then, was the beginning of the "continuing education" or "evening school" idea that would later become a concern of American high schools, colleges, and universities. It is as well an early recognition of the necessity of vocational training. At least one local newspaper looked with favor on the formation of a lyceum in Salem: "The fullness and respectable character of the meeting held last evening to organize a Lyceum for this town, offered ground for the most favorable anticipations, respecting the permanence, utility, and high standing of the institution."[5]

The Salem Lyceum was incorporated on March 4, 1830, but the first lecture was delivered on February 24 by Daniel Appleton White. The title of that lecture, appropriately enough, was "The Advantages of Knowledge." The newspaper notice for this lecture read: "The Salem Lyceum will commence its operation tomorrow evening, under more favorable circumstances than the most sanguine could have anticipated before its formation."[6] The notice anticipated the inadequacy of the lecture hall and saw it as a drawback to the development of the lyceum. The attendance was so large at this first series of lectures, which ended on May 26, that the lyceum had to move from the two small church halls where it had held the lectures to much larger quarters. A new building, constructed at a total cost of about $5,000, was opened on January 19, 1831.[7] By 1832, twenty-three of Essex County's twenty-six towns had lyceums.[8] Salem had one thousand two hundred members in its lyceum at this time as contrasted to a total membership of five thousand five hundred in the twenty-seven best established lyceums in the country. Of these twenty-seven lyceums, Salem was one of the nine or ten that had started to build their own lecture halls.[9] These figures are significant and point to the success and importance of the Salem Lyceum against the larger backdrop of the lyceum movement in Massachusetts and the rest of the country.

Salem was indeed fortunate to have in Henry K. Oliver (a later mayor of Salem) a very early historian of the origin and activities of its lyceum. His *Historical Sketch of the Salem Lyceum* (1879), perhaps the only document of its kind, in addition to explaining some of the lyceum's history, lists all of its officers and all of its lectures. Although some titles and some special lectures are not included, the book provides the scholar with a ready reference for information that would under normal circumstances have to be compiled from newspapers, the minutes of lyceum meetings, and the accounts that were also kept by all lyceums. Since the records of the first twenty years of the Salem Lyceum are now unavailable or lost, Oliver's historical service is invaluable. This information could possibly be gathered from the local newspapers, but they are not, of course, always reliable in this respect.

One of the virtues of the lyceum system was that nearly all lyceums followed the organizational principles that had been established at the beginning of the movement. This uniformity of organization and procedure was convenient not only for the lyceum-goer and lecturer who traveled the circuit but for the student of the movement as well. It was recommended that every lyceum keep minutes of its meetings as well as account books of its financial transactions. A president, vice-president, recording and corresponding secretary, treasurer, and one or more managers were elected in every lyceum. A meeting was held in the fall, usually sometime in September, at which time all those who had paid their dues, generally about two hundred, were allowed to "mark" for lecturers. Presumably, the marking system was a method of checking off the names of those one would like to have lecture before the lyceum for that particular series.[10]

After the marking was done, letters were sent by the corresponding secretary to those who were marked, inviting each to deliver a lecture. These letters of invitation were so similar that a form letter must have been passed down from one corresponding secretary to the next. As a standard procedure the invitation informed the propective lecturer that the rules of the lyceum forbade any lecture of a controversial nature: political, religious, or otherwise. Emerson, for one, so strongly objected to this matter of form that he wrote of it in his *Journals*:

> On the 29 August, I received a letter from the Salem Lyceum signed I. F. Worcester, requesting me to lecture before the institution next winter and adding "The subject is of course discretionary with yourself 'provided no allusions are made to religious controversy, or other exciting topics upon which the public mind is honestly divided.' " I replied on the same day to Mr W. by quoting these words & adding "I am really sorry that any person in Salem should think me capable of accepting an invitation so encumbered."[11]

He followed this entry with " 'The Motto on all palace gates is *Hush.*' " Emerson had lectured before the Salem Lyceum prior to this time,[12] and such letters may not have been used, or he just may not have received the form letter. In either case, the request to abstain from controversial topics was cynically received by Emerson.

As replies to invitations were returned to the secretary, dates were agreed upon and announcements of the forthcoming lectures and often their exact topics, if known in advance, were published in the local newspapers. Tickets for the lyceum were sold at the Lyceum Hall and at several bookstores in Salem, information about the sale of tickets being provided in a large display announcement in the local papers. These tickets were relinquished at the door and admitted men, women who were properly accompanied, and children of at least fourteen years of age. Purchase of tickets for the entire series of lectures was not compulsory; tickets for individual performances cost twenty-five cents and one could choose which performance one wished to attend so that visitors and guests were thus able to be admitted as well. Admission to special series or performances required additional tickets. The lyceum's series usually ended in May, but occasionally, as with Emerson's six lectures on biography, special series were offered in the summer.

The payment that each lecturer was to receive was decided by the directors of the lyceum. It ranged from ten to fifty dollars over the years. Payments were usually uniform during each series, exceptions being made for particularly hard-to-get and very popular lecturers. This fee was usually mentioned in the letter of invitation to lecturers and was fairly standardized from one lyceum to another. Any lyceum that could not pay its lecturers the going rate would have to be one that was grossly undersubscribed or in a town too small to support such an enterprise. The economics of most lyceums was such that they could not only pay their own expenses but, as in the case of the Salem Lyceum, could buy shares in other civic-minded projects and pay for a beautiful new building in a surprisingly short time.[13]

The spirit of the lyceum movement had taken a strong hold on the people of Salem. A "Letter to the Editor" signed by "Fair Play" in the Salem *Register*, October 17, 1850, complained that tickets could not be obtained even after one had supported the Lyceum for twenty-one years. The tickets for the course were sold out by 8:00 A.M. In a diary entry that displays unusual emotion for her, Susan Louise Waters describes an interesting scene at the ticket office of the lyceum:

> I went down to subscribe for Lyceum tickets, I was to get them for several of the girls. The book was open at the Lyceum at 9 oclock, there was quite a crowd around the doors when I went; I got in as far as the entry, but was afraid to push on farther, they had a horrible time. The pressure broke the door down and the Managers had to go off before they had sold quite all their tickets; they had a meeting afterwards and concluded to have two Lyceums different evenings if they could get enough. I did not get any tickets in the first one although two or three tried to get them for me.[14]

Another account describes the character of the two audiences that had actually become necessary much earlier than Susan Waters' account indicates: "Indeed in Salem two courses of lectures became necessary soon after the first series had been delivered, and it was the custom to repeat on Wednesday evening the lecture that had been delivered on Tuesday. For the present day there is a trace of humor in the fact that the Tuesday evening lecture was usually preferred by the Orthodox subscribers, and that of Wednesday by the Unitarians, so that the audiences soon became marked in their sectarian character."[15]

The controversy that Oliver was referring to occurred between 1831 and 1835. The Orthodox group was headed by Rev. John Cheever and the liberal Unitarians by Rev. Charles W. Upham, both of whom carried on their discourses in the local paper. The same Charles W. Upham would, ironically, later be on the conservative side in a different but related theological controversy, in which he would rally to the side of Andrews Norton in the debate over the historical veracity of Christian miracles, a theological battle that Emerson would instigate in his *Divinity School Address* in 1838. This second theological controversy, described and interpreted most readably by William Hutchison in his *The Transcendentalist Ministers: Church Reform in the New England Renaissance*, was the last stand by the Unitarians against the attacks on historical Christianity by the Transcendentalists. The feelings of the common churchgoer and citizen during both of these periods of theological debate must have run high and, as Oliver says, must have caused members of both groups to attend the lyceum on different evenings.

Characterizing audiences is always a problematical undertaking, however. We know that the lyceum was attended by young peole, not all of whom were totally absorbed by the formal proceedings. The lyceum was an acceptable place for young men and women to meet, as Susan Waters' diary shows; she felt that it was more important to record in her diary who escorted her home from the lyceum than to record who lectured there and what was said.[16] The lyceum was also a place where young men could show off by being rowdy and rude. Their behavior embarrassed the town's elders, was a continual subject of letters to the editors of the local papers, and prompted several lyceum resolutions against such disturbances. This rowdyism and the reaction to it as chronicled in the local newspapers forms an interesting little history in itself.[17] Thus, while Oliver has described the two lecture audiences according to their religious preferences, other shaping factors were undoubtedly present; age differences, social factors, and the sincerity of the interest of each audience may also have contributed significantly to Oliver's characterization of them as Orthodox or Unitarian.

However one describes or explains these differing audiences, there appears to be no real evidence that such an audience separation was recognized or regarded as meaningful by lecturers. If such were the case, however, the implications might be far-reaching concerning a figure such as Emerson. Lectures that might have pleased one audience might have offended another, or lectures might have had to be altered to suit the audience on a particular night. We know, of course, that Emerson revised his lectures, but it is extremely difficult to determine what, if anything, the changes he made might indicate about a particular audience.

The Salem lyceum-goers were discriminating. They wanted the best people and they usually got them. They publicly resolved the worth of certain lecturers, mostly foreign ones, and wrote letters to the *Gazette* and *Observer* concerning lectures that were either not factual or violated the rules against controversial topics. The Salemites wanted certain lectures to be repeated and certain lecturers to be invited who were either overlooked or who had lately become available. They also wanted their lyceum tickets to be transferable; that is, they wanted tickets that could be used by more than one member of the family. The Salem lyceum-goers were embarrassed by rowdiness, people who talked during lectures, and latecomers who crashed about in their attempts to find seats, and they resolved not to allow such disturbances. Salemites were always conscious of what Boston was doing, and they became annoyed if Boston attracted a lecturer they could not get. This fact, in turn, placed a great deal of stress on the lyceum managers as well as on the secretary. Nathaniel Hawthorne, one of the two most famous of all the lyceum corresponding secretaries (the other being Henry David Thoreau of the Concord Lyceum), seems not to have withstood the rigors of his assignment with any great enthusiasm. He writes to Thoreau imploring him to lecture in Salem and adds a revealing note:

Boston, Nov 20th, 1848

My dear Thoreau,
  I did not sooner write you, because there were preen-gagements for the two or three first lectures, so that I could not arrange matters to have you come during the present month. But, as it happens, the expected lectures have failed us; and we now depend on you to come this very next Wednesday. I shall announce you in the paper of tomorrow, so you *must* come. I regret that I could not give you longer notice.
  We shall expect you on Wednesday, at No 14 Mall. Street.

Yours truly,
Nath Hawthorne.

  If it is utterly impossible for you to come, pray write me a line so that I may get it Wednesday morning. But, by all means, come.
  This Secretaryship is an intolerable bore. I have travelled thirty miles, this wet day for no other business.[18]

Both the number of lectures in each series and the number of series itself given by the Salem Lyceum is impressive. During the first fifty series, 853 lectures were given. Among the lecturers were many prominent Salemites including: Rufus Choate, Samuel Johnson, Jr., Henry K. Oliver, Francis Peabody, Abel L. Peirson, Charles W. Upham, Jones Very, and Jonathan Webb. Those men who came from outside Salem and who helped make the Salem Lyceum a success were some of the brightest luminaries of the age—an awesome congregation of great thinkers and eloquent speakers:

Charles Francis Adams
John Quincy Adams
Louis Agassiz
George Bancroft
Clara Barton
Henry Ward Beecher
Alexander Graham Bell
Orestes Brownson
Anson Burlingame
George Catlin
William Henry Channing
James Freeman Clark
Moncure Daniel Conway
George William Curtis
Caleb Cushing
Richard Henry Dana, Jr.

Ralph Waldo Emerson
Edward Everett
James T. Fields
Octavius Brooks
    Frothingham
William Lloyd Garrison
Sylvester Graham
Frederic H. Hedge
Thomas Wentworth Higginson
Oliver Wendell Holmes
Mark Hopkins
H. N. Hudson
Sylvester Judd, Jr.
James Russell Lowell

Horace Mann
Charles Eliot Norton
Theodore Parker
Andrew Preston Peabody
Wendell Phillips
Carl Schurz
Jared Sparks
Charles Sumner
Bayard Taylor
Henry David Thoreau
James Walker
Daniel Webster
Robert C. Winthrop[19]

The Salem Lyceum reached its peak about the middle of the nineteenth century; the twenty-sixth course (1854–1855) given by the lyceum gives some idea of the caliber of intellectual entertainment that it made available to every citizen:

Germania Serenade Band . . Concert
Joseph P. Thompson (2) . . . . Constantinople
                              Jerusalem and Damascus
Josiah Quincy, Jr. . . . . Sectional Prejudices
Thomas W. Higginson . . . . . The Old Puritan Clergyman
Louis Agassiz . . . . The Animal Kingdom
Reignold Solger . . . . The Present State of the
                              Eastern Question
Thomas Russell . . . . Influence of Character on National Destiny
George F. Simmons . . . . The Eastern War
W. H. Hurlbut . . . . The Middle Ages
Charles L. Brace (2) . . . . The Principalities of Europe
                              Ragged Schools
Henry Ward Beecher . . . . . Patriotism
Thomas T. Stone (2) . . . . . Rise and Fall of the Roman Empire
                              Peasants' War in Germany

John Pierpont (2)	Education
	Moral Influence of Physical Science
Theodore Parker (2)	The Anglo Saxon
	The Condition, Character, and Prospects of America
George W. Curtis	Success
George R. Russell	The Politician
W. H. Ryder	Ancient and Modern Civilization
R. C. Waterson	Switzerland
James Russell Lowell (2) . . .	Edmund Spenser
	Analysis of Poetry
Ralph Waldo Emerson (2) . .	Fruits of English Civilization
	French Character
Richard H. Dana, Jr.	Sources of Influence[20]

In 1888 the Lyceum Building was razed.[21] The loss of the building symbolized the greater loss of that spirit of inquiry that had served the lyceum so admirably over the years.

On January 24, 1898, the Salem Lyceum was officially closed and its records were passed on to the Essex Institute, which, in 1929, began a series of lectures marking the one-hundredth anniversary of the Salem Lyceum. The Essex Institute was also the recipient of the lyceum fund, a fitting transfer of money and activities since the Institute had carried on its own lectures in Plummer Hall even before the lyceum had closed down. Indeed the Plummer Hall lecture series could boast that on February 12, 1877, Professor Alexander Graham Bell delivered a lecture about the telephone and the news of that lecture was delivered by telephone to the *Boston Globe* where it appeared the next day.[22]

The history, structure, and activities of the Salem Lyceum do not in themselves tell us much about Transcendentalism, but they do tell us a great deal about Salem and are necessary elements in a picture of a changing town and its people. What remains to be told is the story of the role that Transcendentalism played in the lyceum movement, and for that we must turn chiefly to the relationship of Ralph Waldo Emerson and the lyceum. Although Emerson was a vital link in that relationship, he did not stand alone and for this reason other figures also receive some attention here.

After Emerson resigned from the Second Church (October 28, 1832) and spent eleven months (December 1832–October 1833) traveling in Europe, he returned to the United States where within a few weeks he began to lecture. Any measure of Emerson's platform success has to take into account his relationship to his audience. Emerson himself believed that the civic leader held great power over the people in the community because he was at home there, knew its inhabitants, and could lead them by strength of character and power of statement. Emerson was far from possessing any of these characteristics at the beginning of his lecturing career. He was quiet, contemplative, and uneasy in forced social situations. A childhood disease prevented him from exhibiting great energy or vitality in the usual sense, and the recent direction in which his mind had taken him placed him at odds with the rest of the community. All the reasons, exclusive of theological ones, that had driven Emerson from the pulpit seemed to spell disaster for him on the lecture platform. Emerson finally found the right relationship to his audience by going completely his own way, by remaining very much aloof, and by releasing himself from any ordinary intellectual responsibility to his audience.[23]

Eventually, Emerson cut a fine figure on the lecture platform and that figure had much to do with the effectiveness of his lectures in general. The Cincinnati *Gazette* gave a detailed description of Emerson's appearance when he lectured there on January 27, 1857:

> Mr. Emerson is a tall man, full six feet high, but slender and bony, and in his plain suit of ill-fitting black, looked not unlike a New England country schoolmaster. His face is thin and strongly marked, his nose large, and his eye-

brows highly arched and meeting. He rarely looks his hearers
full in the face, but at emphatic expressions has a habit
of turning his eyes backward as though he desired to look
in at himself. His voice is like his sentences—not smooth
nor even, yet occasionally giving a tone of considerable
sweetness, and he has an auracular [sic] way of delivering
himself that is calculated to impress the audience.

When introduced to the audience he stood straight up,
exhibiting his tall form—then looked down bashfully at
the manuscript in his hand—then advanced rather ungrace-
fully to the stand, and with an appearance of embarrassment,
and in a half apologetic, introductory tone, began . . .
Gentlemen and Ladies.[24]

In describing a series of famous literary figures, another newspaper writer said of Emerson that "he looks like a refined
farmer, meditative and quiet."[25]

It was a happy coincidence that Emerson's life took a new
direction at the time of the inception and growth of the lyceum
movement. It was more than chance, however, that he should
further his interest in science at a time when everyone was
in search of practical and scientific knowledge. He lectured
on "The Uses of Natural History." Emerson characteristi-
cally gave his audiences what they wanted but in the way
that he wanted them to have it. He wrote in his journal: "Do,
dear, when you come to write Lyceum lectures, remember
that you are not to say, What must be said in a Lyceum? but
what discoveries or stimulating thoughts have I to impart
to a thousand persons? not what they will expect to hear but
what is fit for me to say."[26] Emerson was not interested in
scientific cataloging, classification, or observation. Neither
was he interested in the more useful applications of scientific
knowledge. Emerson's primary interest was in what these
actions and science could tell man of his unique position
in the universe. He gave the human and transcendent side
of science and, although some scientists were opposed to
what he had to say, the audiences as a whole were enthralled.[27]

The day after Emerson delivered what might be called his first American lecture, which had been arranged for him by his brother Charles and his cousin George Emerson, who was active very early in the lyceum movement, Charles wrote to William Emerson concerning Waldo's performance: " 'Last Evening Waldo lectured before the Nat. Hist. Soc. to a charm. The young & old opened their eyes & their ears—I was glad to have some of the stump lecturers see what was what & how to the rising sun . . . .' "[28] Shortly after Emerson began to lecture, he returned to the Second Church for the solemn duty of delivering a funeral oration on the death of his friend George Sampson, and it was at this time that A. Bronson Alcott and Elizabeth Palmer Peabody had an opportunity to hear him. Elizabeth Peabody said that words could hardly do justice to the tribute that Emerson paid Sampson: "His expression—his tones—his prayers—his readings of Scripture— his sermon . . . will live in my soul forever & ever—And *I Know that man* as well as I could have known him had I been his acquaintance on earth."[29] It is difficult to say whether people were much affected by Emerson's Transcendentalism; clearly they were much impressed by his manner.

Emerson expressed his attitude toward lecturing in Salem indirectly. Several years after Emerson began to lecture, he wrote Thomas Carlyle concerning the prospect of Carlyle's earning an income by lecturing should his proposed American visit materialize: "If the lectures succeed in Boston, their success is insured at Salem, a town thirteen miles off, with a population of 15,000."[30] In another letter indicating the importance of Salem's lyceum and how enthusiastic lyceum audiences were even as early as 1835, Emerson tells Carlyle that if his lectures were to be enthusiastically received, the Boston-Salem-Cambridge area lyceums could insure him a solid foundation for a reasonable income.[31]

Charles Emerson, Waldo's brother, had lectured before the Salem Lyceum in 1835 on the topic of "Socrates." This lecture and the presence in Salem of the influential Charles

Wentworth Upham, a college friend but also a man who would very soon turn against Emerson, as well as the fact that Salem had heard of Emerson's successes in Boston and in characteristic fashion wanted him to lecture in Salem in order to evaluate him firsthand—all worked toward bringing Emerson and Salem together. Salem, which was no farther from Concord than Boston, was also convenient for Emerson. Emerson appeared before lyceum audiences in Salem over forty times and they seemed never to tire of him. The frequency of his Salem lectures attests to the high regard that the Salemites had for him.

The Salem *Gazette*, in a reprint from the *National Intelligencer*, gives this response to Emerson's lectures: "Emerson, the transcendentalist, lectures very beautifully, and as he is a kind of beloved-apostle looking man, the ladies run after him a great deal."[32] The essence of these descriptions is found in varying degrees in all accounts of Emerson's lyceum appearances. He never altered his manner on the platform and as he relied on no tricks, physical or oratorical, his ability to captivate an audience always remains somewhat mysterious. The following is a chronology of Emerson's Salem lectures.[33]

Date	Title
January 18 (?), 1836	"Biography" series: probably
February 17, 1836	"Introduction" and "Michel
February 28, 1836	Angelo Buonaroti," "John
March 1, 1836	Milton," "George Fox," and
	"Edmund Burke"
March 2, 1836	"Martin Luther"
April 18, 1836	Six lectures on "English Biography and Literature," No. 1
April 20, 1836	No. 2
May 2, 1836	No. 3
May 4, 1836	No. 4
May 6, 1836	No. 5
May 7, 1836	No. 6
(?) March 7, 1837	not available
March 20, 1837	not available

February 17, 1840	not available
February 26 or 27, 1840	"Analysis, the Character of the Present Age"
January 10, 1844	"The New England Man"
March 6, 1844	"Want of Distinctive National Character"
December 11, 1844	"Genius of the New Englander"
March 25, 1846	"Napoleon"
February 17, 1847	"Eloquence"
January 17, 1849	"England and the English"
1849–1850	"Traits of the Times"
January 21, 1851	"Law of Success"
January 8, 1852	Probably "Economy"
March 8, 1852	Probably "Fate"
November 29, 1853	"American Character"
1854–1855	"Fruits of English Civilization"
March 14, 1855	"French Character"
December 25 and 26, 1855	"Beauty"
(?) January 29, 1856	not available
February 10 (?), 1856	"Works and Days"
February 11, 1857	"Works and Days"
January 20, 1858	"Finer Relations of Man to Nature"
November 4, 1858	Five lectures: "Conduct of Life" series, No. 1
November 9, 1858	No. 2
November 11, 1858	No. 3
November 16, 1858	No. 4
November 18, 1858	No. 5
December 29, 1858	"Good in Evil" and "Conduct of Life"
January 6, 1860	"John Brown"
January 11, 1860	"Manners"
December 19, 1860	"Clubs"
November 27, 1861	"Old Age"
November 19, 1862	"Perpetual Forces"
1863–1864	"The True American Idea"
January 27, 1864	"Fortune of the Republic"

January 4, 1865	"Social Aims"
1865–1866	"Social Forces"
January 3, 1866	"Resources"
December 19, 1866	"Man of the World"
January 29, 1868	"Eloquence"
January 13, 1869	"Brook Farm"
February 16, 1870	"Courage"
February 15, 1871	"Homes and Hospitality"

Emerson's early lectures are perhaps his most important ones, for it is in these lectures that the development of his Transcendental ideas can be seen most clearly. His earliest lectures were the four on science: "The Uses of Natural History," "On the Relation of Man to the Globe," "Water," and "The Naturalist." Although we do not know definitely, it is probable that some of Emerson's earliest Salem lectures were on scientific subjects. In the "Natural History" series Emerson lists many reasons for studying natural history, the most important of which is that such study can explain mankind itself. It is here that Emerson begins to put forth the metaphysical idea of correspondence, "that correspondence of the outward world to the inward world of thoughts and emotions,"[34] of the Understanding, and the unity of all things—ideas that would see their fullest expression in *Nature*. Throughout these lectures on science Emerson formulated ideas that established the foundation of his later beliefs. He had to do enough scientific study to prove that his beliefs were accurate. When he was assured that he was on the right track, he changed the direction and emphasis of his studies.

In his next series of six lectures on biography, Emerson moved away from his concern for science. The lyceum was satisfied to see science as an end in itself; Emerson wanted to move science from the world of Understanding to the world of Reason or at least to see Understanding and Reason as being of equal importance. He writes in his journal: "I would learn the law of the diffraction of a ray because, when I understand it, it will illustrate, perhaps suggest a new truth in ethics."[35]

He found the science lectures too time-consuming and too reliant on the work of others, but, in general, he felt they served his purposes well.

Throughout these lectures on science Emerson relied on the writings of important scientists, from history as well as his own day, to such an extent that the qualities of personal genius began to interest him. The general public in Emerson's time, as in all ages, was interested in the aspects of personality that lift certain men out of the ranks of the ordinary and into the world's eye. Local newspapers of Emerson's day contain many accounts of the personalities, idiosyncracies, and life-styles of great people, and once again he fitted his personal interests to those of the public at large.

The "Biography" series ("Introduction," "Michel Angelo Buonaroti," "John Milton," "George Fox," "Edmund Burke," and "Martin Luther") was given during January, February, and March of 1836 at the request of Upham. The lecture on Michelangelo sought more than anything else to put forth the picture of a well-directed life, a life whose total objective was the creation of Beauty. Emerson tells the workers, the farmers, the laborers, and the mechanics in his audience that because the subject of his lecture is the Beautiful they should not feel that it is alien to them. Emerson tells the audience that Michelangelo's creation of Beauty was very much dependent on his intimate understanding of the mechanical arts. Michelangelo had studied physics, the workings of the human body, and the principles of architecture, which were so reliant upon knowledge of the elements of engineering. Moreover, Michelangelo worked incessantly and untiringly toward the perfection of his art. Workers, thought Emerson, do not always understand the beauty of their work and he believed that he could indicate to them just how important their jobs were. Some of the ideas expressed in "Michel Angelo" found their way into the section on Beauty in *Nature*. Michelangelo's search for Beauty led him beyond his goal: "Therefore as in the first place he sought to approach the Beautiful by study of the True, so he failed not to make the next stop of progress and to seek Beauty in the highest form, that of Goodness."[36] Michelangelo's soul was "enamoured of grace" and the total picture here is one of a gradual movement toward the godly. In his search for Beauty, Michelangelo and his work had transcended this world and had approached the spiritual idea of Beauty.

Here, as in all of Emerson's biographical lectures, one is surprised by the parallels between what these men of whom Emerson spoke believed and what Emerson himself believed. To be sure, Emerson went to these men because he liked what he saw, but he also saw what he liked in them. In Michelangelo Emerson found a great concern for beauty; in Luther, a preoccupation with the pursuit of truth; in Fox, light and inspiration; and in Burke, the rare combination of thought and action in one man. In short, the impression one gets is that Emerson is often talking about himself in these lectures. Each man he speaks of is the perfection of at least one of the traits that we now realize were beginning to characterize Emerson himself.

The Science and Biography series, like the series on English literature that Emerson delivered next before the Society for the Diffusion of Useful Knowledge at the Masonic Temple in Boston, are interesting revelations of his reflections at the time and they are important because parts of them found their way into *Nature* and were the last important lectures before the writing of that work. Had Emerson never written *Nature* he would have in the Science, Biography, and Literature series revealed the essence of Transcendentalism as he conceived it. *Nature* was then the climactic gathering of essential ideas that were quite diverse in their origins; it was, moreover, an impassioned and artful presentation of those ideas.

In the spring of 1836, Emerson delivered six (it is not known which) of the ten English literature lectures before the Salem Lyceum. These lectures were not well attended initially.

Emerson writes to his wife Lidian the day after the first lecture and reveals his disappointment:

> I found as might be expected last evening some shortcoming of such golden promises. About 130 tickets to 150 had been sold. Mr Upham had been confined at home with a cold & thinks proper care had not been taken in advertising, &c. by Dr Peabody who seems to manage the matter, father of E. P. P. All agreed however in saying that more would come. Perhaps some more will. This is quite as large a company as I think the lectures can naturally command in this town, and so I shall be surprized if many more should attend.[37]

Before Emerson could better ascertain how willing audiences were to hear him he was called away from the series by the illness of his brother Charles, who would die shortly thereafter. He returned to deliver the rest of his lectures but no record of attendance at those lectures is available. Late in April, however, the Salem *Observer* printed the following comment:

Mr. Emerson's Lectures

> If we are not much mistaken in our estimation, Mr. Emerson invests his lectures with a peculiar and strong charm. There are few subjects in the range of human contemplation that possess a more general interest than the biography of eminent persons who have lived and gone before us. There is a strong desire to look into the characters of those who have effected great purposes in life;—we are anxious to know something of the peculiar structure of their minds, of the prominent and distinctive points of their characters,— of their everyday habits and ordinary modes of expression and intercourse;—to discover, if possible, in what way they differed from the general and monotonous mass of men. Even the characters of those who have made themselves famous by strong, but wicked deeds, come in for a share of this interest. To give the outlines of a character, in the course of one short lecture, in such a manner as to

forcibly suggest the whole structure,—to select from the
mass of records of great lives, such traits and facts as tend
most clearly and directly to develope character is no ordinary art. Mr. Emerson appears to possess the faculty
in an eminent degree. From the scattered fragments of
character he seems to know exactly what to choose and
how to combine wherewithal to recreate and present a
living semblance to the eye of the mind. The manner of
the lecturer is such as veils the effort and art of oratory,
and is therefore very effective.[38]

Emerson delivered the first lecture in the special series
on April 18, 1836. The date of this item (he had delivered
only one lecture by then) and its contents (praising as it does
Emerson's ability to revitalize historical figures) reveals that
this review was based upon Emerson's Biography series and
that it was well received. It is known for certain that he delivered his "Martin Luther" lecture in Salem but it seems
likely that he gave the whole of the series there.

On February 23, 1838, the Salem *Gazette* advertised a
lecture on Transcendentalism to be given by Rev. James
Walker of Charlestown, whose philosophic attitude must have
been clear by 1834. Octavius B. Frothingham said of Walker's
inclination to Transcendentalism: "In 1834, James Walker
printed in the 'Christian Examiner' an address, which was
the same year published as a tract, by the American Unitarian Association, entitled 'The Philosophy of Man's Spiritual
Nature in regard to the foundations of Faith,' wherein he took
frankly the transcendental ground, contending:

'That the existence of those spiritual faculties and capacities which are assumed as the foundation of religion
in the soul of man, is attested, and put beyond controversy
by the revelations of consciousness; that religion in the
soul, consisting as it does, of a manifestation and development of these spiritual faculties and capacities, is as much
a reality in itself, and enters as essentially into our idea

of a perfect man, as the corresponding manifestation and development of the reasoning faculties, a sense of justice, or the affections of sympathy and benevolence; and that 'from the acknowledged existence and reality of spiritual impressions or perceptions, we may and do assume the existence and reality of the spiritual world; just as from the acknowledged existence and reality of sensible impressions or perceptions, we may and do assume the existence and realities of the sensible world.' "[39]

A further connection between Walker and Transcendentalism is revealed by the fact that in 1836 he was invited to the initial meeting of the Transcendental Club or Symposium.[40] Within two weeks of that February 1838 lecture in Salem Walker was appointed to the faculty of Harvard's religion department, and he was later to become president of Harvard (1853–56). Elizabeth Palmer Peabody who attended Walker's lecture did not like all that she heard or thought she heard and in her own inimitable way sought to clarify her impressions: "I have just heard Mr. Walker's lecture which is grand— Only I cannot understand why he refuses to name the transcendental facts he affirms to exist—*innate ideas* and I am *afraid* he made some backhanded thrusts at Carlyle & Mr. Emerson. But I shall see him tomorrow & inquire into it."[41]

On March 2, 1838, the Salem *Gazette* reprinted a review of Walker's lecture that had appeared in the *Christian Register*. It was not a review of the actual Salem performance but the contents of the review indicate that it was on the same lecture. The review itself does not seem to validate Miss Peabody's concern; it does, however, do something much more important. The review put before the people of Salem the major tenets of Transcendental thought at a time when they were still being formulated in the minds of the movement's prime movers. The following is a copy of that review in its entirety.

TRANSCENDENTALISM

The Lecture of Rev. Dr. Walker, on this subject, before the Society for the Diffusion of Useful Knowledge, on Friday evening 9th inst. was an admirable specimen of profound philosophical discussion, conducted with such simplicity and clearness, as to make it intelligible and attractive to the numerous audience, to which it was addressed. We were greatly struck with the scientific rigor and exactness which were sustained throughout the lecture; but perhaps not less so with the felicitous skill with which some of the most difficult points of speculation were brought within the grasp of the common understanding.

Some words, said Dr. Walker, affect the mind on account of what they mean; others, on account of what they suggest. Of this last class, the word Transcendentalism is one of the most conspicuous. It is uttered much oftener than understood. It is no sooner pronounced than it awakens in many minds, the idea of extravagant opinions, wild and rash speculations, and all that is objectionable and offensive in German metaphysics and mysticism.

This, however, is an error, proceeding from a misapprehension of the real significance of the term, and from ignorance of the course of philosophic inquiry for the last three quarters of a century. The father of the Transcendental philosophy was a man of the most extensive attainments in science; of singular logical acuteness:—with no love of innovation; but one of the most sincere, earnest, and vigorous inquirers after truth, whose names are preserved in the history of letters. This was Immanuel Kant, the philosopher of Konigsberg.

It is said that the writings of Kant are difficult of comprehension by the English student; and this allegation was admitted and accounted for by the Lecturer. It rose partly from the fact that the philosophical culture with which we start is widely different from that of Kant, when he first proposed the Transcendental problem. We usually commence with Locke and the English metaphysicians; we are familiar with their points of view; we understand their nomenclature; and we are able to follow with ease, the discussions which are founded on their principles. Kant on the contrary, had been formed in the school of Descartes and of Leibnitz; he is sailing, so to speak, in a different direction from that to which we are accustomed; he uses a different chart; he refers to different bearings; and we are of course perplexed in our first endeavors to follow him. But whatever be the obscurity of Kant, it is not the obscurity of a mystic, of a loose reasoner, of a cloudy thinker, of a man who fails to be understood by others, because he does not understand himself. It is far more analogous to the obscurity of Bishop Butler, which arises from the compactness of his argument, than to that of Jacob Boehmen, which proceeds from vague, inconsistent and confused perceptions of truth.

The Transcendental problem as it was called by Mr Walker, was traced back to the philosophy of Bacon and Locke. The radical error of Mr Locke's system was stated to be its empyrical character, that is, the denial of all knowledge that is not founded on experience. This principle fully unfolded led to the scepticism of Hume. The consequences drawn by Mr Hume from the supposition that all our knowledge is obtained from experience, without admitting that portion which is derived from the mind itself, prior to the experience, and which is the essential condition of the possibility of experience, cut away, at a blow, the ground of all belief, all human convictions, all certainty of knowledge, and in fact all the investigations of science in every department whatever.

The question then arose, what part of our knowledge is founded on the inherent nature of the mind itself, independent of actual experience. This was answered by Dr. Reid, with his first truths established by the testimony of common sense; and by Dugald Stewart, with his fundamental laws of human belief. The labors of Kant were devoted to the solution of the same problem. The result of his investigations, which were in the same direction with those of the Scottish philosophers, but more profound, more systematic, more rigid, was the Transcendental philosophy. Transcendentalism, therefore, is the scientific establishment of the principles of common sense, in opposition to the scepticism of David Hume.

The lecture was closed with an eloquent exposition of the value and advantages of the Transcendental philosophy, considered in the point of view in which it has been presented, as the endeavor of reason to comprehend itself, and to legitimate and strengthen the primitive convictions of the human mind.

The tendency of this philosophy, Dr. Walker maintained, was to establish the authority of justice and conscience against the inroads of a selfish and worldly expediency; to quicken the principle of faith in the great spiritual truths, which are the glory and consolation of our nature; and to destroy the morbid and puny mysticism, which sometimes usurps the name of philosophy, but which is at war with its essential spirit and purposes. Even this mystic sentimentalism however, is entitled to tolerance, as it indicates the great want of times, namely, a deeper, more vital, more comprehensive exhibition of truth; a system which shall do justice to the whole nature of man, and aid and inspire him in his holiest endeavors. The want of such a system cannot be kept out of sight.—The enthusiasm, which impelled by a noble and generous love of truth, seeks to arrive at it, cannot be crushed. It can be satisfied only with a sound, spiritual, Eclectic philosophy, which shall reconcile the claims of Transcendentalism and of common sense; and put an end to the separation of ideas, which are in reality one.

Christian Register[42]

There were other lecturers and lectures at the Salem Lyceum that were either Transcendental in nature or showed a strong inclination in that direction. As early as the seventh course (1836), a young Unitarian minister, William Silsbee, delivered a lecture entitled "Aesthetic Culture,"[43] which followed Emerson's "Martin Luther." As he begins, Silsbee sounds very much like Emerson; he informs his audience that he is aware of the fact that his topic might not seem appropriate for a lyceum audience. He fears that many might think that something more practical might be more beneficial. He answers: "Nay, it is to be feared there are some, who are ready with the epithet 'speculative' or 'theatrical,' to condemn whatever has not the most direct bearing upon their physical welfare."[44] Silsbee then goes on in an Emersonian prose style to justify his discussion of the unreal, visionary, faithful, and ideal. The age is so utilitarian, so mechanically, practically, and scientifically minded, he says, that a concern for the beautiful and for aesthetics is certainly in order. The following is an example of Silsbee's Emersonian sensibility and expression:

> ... it may not at least be *taken for granted* that there is nothing nobler than for a man to walk about this earth with prone eyes like the brutes that perish, forgetting that his erect posture was given to look around and above, and beyond him—so long too, it may not be claimed for the highest wisdom to see in the mighty cataract only so much "water power," in the noble views which traverse our land, only so many means of easy intercourse; and to look upon the vast Ocean itself—that symbol of the Infinite—as but a convenient highway, whereupon our ships may the sooner bring home the gainful products of other climes.[45]

Silsbee had been told that his topic and general concerns as well as his expression of them was very much in line with Emerson's own ideas, and the comparison must have been bothersome enough to Silsbee because he expressed a desire to meet Emerson. On October 1, 1838, however, Silsbee wrote to Emerson to ask him some questions about prayers, God, miracles, and the new movement, Transcendentalism. Emerson answered the young minister on October 4, 1838, and copied the letter into his journal:

> —I read in your letter the expressions of an earnest character of faith, of hope, with extreme interest; and if I can contribute any aid by sympathy or suggestion to the solution of the great problems that occupy you, I shall be glad. But I think it must be done by degrees. I am not sufficiently master of the little truth I see, to know how to state it in forms so general as shall put every mind in possession of my point of view. We generalize and rectify our expressions by continual efforts from day to day, from month to month, to reconcile our own sight with that of our companions. So shall two inquirers have the best mutual action on each other. But I should never attempt a direct answer to such

questions as yours. I have no language that could shortly present my state of mind in regard to each of them with any fidelity; for my state of mind on each is nowise final and detached, but tentative, progressive, and strictly connected with the whole circle of my thoughts. It seems to me that to understand any man's thoughts respecting the Supreme Being, we need an insight into the general habit and tendency of his speculations; for, every man's idea of God is the last or most comprehensive generalization at which he has arrived.—But besides the extreme difficulty of stating our results on such questions in a few propositions, I think, my dear sir, that a certain religious feeling deters us from the attempt. I do not gladly utter any deep convictions of the soul in any company where I think it will be contested, no, nor unless I think it will be welcome. Truth has already ceased to be itself if polemically said; and if the soul would utter oracles, as every soul should, it must live for itself, keep itself right-minded,— observe with such awe its own law as to concern itself very little with the engrossing topics of the hour, unless they be its own. I believe that most of the speculative difficulties which infest us, we must thank ourselves for; each mind, if true to itself, will, by living forthright, and not importing into it the doubts of other men, dissolve all difficulties, as the sun at midsummer burns up the clouds. Hence I think the aid we can give each other is only incidental, lateral, and sympathetic. If we are true and benevolent, we reenforce each other by every act and word. Your heroism stimulates mine; your light kindles mine. At the end of all this is, that I thank you heartily for the confidence of your letter, and beg you to use your earliest leisure to come and see me. It is very possible that I shall not be able to give you one definition, but I will show you with joy what I strive after and what I worship, as far as I can. Meantime, I shall be very glad to hear from you by letter.[46]

Silsbee evidently was not satisfied by Emerson's honest and sympathetic reply and he consequently wrote to Theodore Parker for those answers that Emerson was unwilling to supply him.[47] Silsbee, who may have been a relative of Mary Anne Silsbee and in the circle of the little-known but very influential

Susan Burley of Salem, did, however, fall under the watchful eye of Elizabeth Palmer Peabody. Peabody verifies Silsbee's
philosophic attitude in a letter to Emerson: "On reading your
Cambridge address, he [Silsbee] said he understood it *all* and
liked it *all*—and so there was no excuse to go."[48]

On October 21, 1848, Nathaniel Hawthorne wrote the
following letter to Henry David Thoreau requesting that
Thoreau lecture before the Salem Lyceum:

My dear Sir,

   The Managers of the Salem Lyceum, some time ago,
voted that you should be requested to deliver a Lecture
before that Institution, during the approaching season.
I know not whether Mr Chever, the late corresponding
Secretary, communicated the vote to you; at all events,
no answer has been received, and, as Mr Chever's successor
in office, I am instructed to repeat the invitation. Permit
me to add my own earnest wishes that you will accept
it—and also, laying aside my official dignity, to express
my wife's desire and my own that you will be our guest,
if you do come.
   In case of your compliance, the Managers would be
glad to know at what time it will best suit you to deliver
the Lecture.

Very truly Yours,
Nathl Hawthorne,
Cor. Secy Salem Lyceum.

P.S. I live at No 14, Mall Street—where I shall be very
happy to see you. The stated fee for Lectures is $20.[49]

Being relatively unknown at the time, Thoreau did not
fare well at the hands of the Salem *Observer*, which announced
him as "Henry S. Thoreau, Of Concord, N.H."[50] Since he
was unknown, however, it was unusual for the press to pay
Thoreau as much notice as it did. He was given an extended
review that stressed, its disclaimers notwithstanding, more
the power of Emerson's friendship than any native talent

or original thinking on Thoreau's part. The following is the account of what was probably Thoreau's first lecture outside of Concord:

Mr. Thoreau, of Concord, gave his auditors a lecture on Wednesday evening, sufficiently *Emersonian* to have come from the great philosopher himself. We were reminded of Emerson continually. In thought, style and delivery, the similarity was equally obvious. There was the same keen philosophy running through him, the same jutting forth of "brilliant edges of meaning" as Gilfillan has it. Even in tone of voice, Emerson was brought strikingly to the ear; and, in personal appearance also, we fancied some little resemblance. The close likeness between the two would almost justify a charge of plagiarism, were it not that Mr. Thoreau's lecture furnished ample proof of being a native product, by affording all the charm of an original. Rather than an imitation of Emerson, it was the unfolding of a like mind with his; as if the two men had grown in the same soil and under the same culture.

The reader may remember having recently seen an article from the N.Y. Tribune, describing the recluse life led by a scholar, who supported himself by manual labor, and on a regime which cost only *twenty-seven cents a week*, making it necessary to labor but six weeks to provide sufficient of the necessaries of life to serve the balance of the year. Mr. Thoreau is the hero of that story—although he claims no heroism, considering himself simply an economist.

The subject of this lecture was Economy, illustrated by the experiment mentioned.—This was done in an admirable manner, in a strain of exquisite humor, with a strong under current of delicate satire against the follies of the times. Then there were interspersed observations, speculations, and suggestions upon dress, fashions, food, dwellings, furniture, etc., etc., sufficiently queer to keep the audience in almost constant mirth, and sufficiently wise and new to afford many good practical hints and precepts.

The performance has created "quite a sensation" amongst the Lyceum goers.[51]

The first lecture that Thoreau delivered to the Salem Lyceum was entitled "Student Life in New England, its Economy."[52] This lecture was a draft of the opening chapter or chapters of *Walden*. The exact relationship between the lecture and *Walden* is not clear.[53] The review, in stating that it was "Emersonian" and philosophic, and the title, which more than hints of the first chapter of *Walden*, seem to indicate that the lecture was typically Thoreauvian in style and content.

Sophia Hawthorne gives an account of her impressions of Thoreau's lecture:

> "This evening Mr. Thoreau is going to lecture, and will stay with us. His lecture before was so enchanting; such a revelation of nature in all its exquisite details of wood-thrushes, squirrels, sunshine, mists and shadows, fresh, vernal odors, pine-tree ocean melodies, that my ear rang with music, and I seem to have been wandering through copse and dingle! Mr. Thoreau has risen above all his arrogance of manner, and is as gentle, simple, ruddy, and meek as all geniuses should be! And now his great blue eyes fairly outshine and put into shade a nose which I once thought must make him uncomely forever."[54]

Thoreau's second lecture, "Student Life, its Aims and Employments," was also delivered during the twentieth course (1848–49) of the Salem Lyceum.[55] Hawthorne wrote to Thoreau on February 19, 1849:

My dear Thoreau,

The managers request that you will lecture before the Salem Lyceum on Wednesday evening *after* next—that is to say, on the 28th inst. May we depend on you? Please to answer immediately, if convenient.

Mr. Alcott delighted my wife and me, the other evening, by announcing that you had a book in prep. I rejoice at it, and nothing doubt of such success as will be worth having. Should your manuscripts all be in the printer's hands, I suppose you can reclaim one of them, for a single evening's use, to be returned the next morning; or perhaps that Indian lecture, which you mentioned to me, is in a state of forwardness. Either that, or a continuation of the Walden experiment (or, indeed, anything else.) will be acceptable. We shall expect you at 14 Mall Street.

Very truly yours,
Nathl Hawthorne.[56]

The review of Thoreau's second lecture indicates that perhaps the lecturer was a little too Thoreauvian and not practical enough for the audience. There is reference to "tom-foolery and nonsense," to a difference of opinion between the more and the less practical members of the audience, and to what it is fitting for a popular audience to hear. The review must have been only an indication of the audience's larger discontent, for Thoreau was never again invited to lecture before the Salem Lyceum.

MR. THOREAU, of Concord, delivered a second lecture on Wednesday evening upon his life in the woods. The first lecture was upon the economy of that life; this was upon its object and some of its enjoyments. Judging from the remarks which we have heard concerning it, Mr. Thoreau was even less successful this time in suiting all, than on the former occasion. The diversity of opinion is quite amusing. Some persons are unwilling to speak of his lecture as any better than "tom-foolery and nonsense," while others think they perceived, beneath the outward sense of his remarks, something wise and valuable. It is undoubtedly true that Mr. Thoreau's style is rather too allegorical for a popular audience. He "peoples the solitudes" of the woods too profusely, and gives voices to their "dim aisles" not recognized by the larger part of common ears.

Some parts of this lecture—which on the whole we thought less successful than the former one—were generally admitted to be excellent. He gave a well-considered defence of classical literature, in connection with some common sense remarks upon books; and also some ingenious speculations suggested by the inroads of railroad enterprise upon the quiet and seclusion of Walden Pond; and told how he found nature a counsellor and companion, furnishing

"Tongues in the trees, books in the running brooks, Sermons in stones, and good in everything."

We take the purpose of Mr. T's lecture to have been, the elucidation of the poetical view of life—showing how life may be made poetical, the apprehensive imagination clothing all things with divine forms, and gathering from them a divine language.

"He went to the gods of the wood To bring their word to me."

And here we may remark that the public are becoming more critical. The standard of Lyceum lectures has been raised very considerably within a few years, and lecturers who would have given full satisfaction not long since, are "voted bores" at present. This is certainly a good indication, and shows that Lyceums have accomplished an important work. We doubt if twenty years ago such lecturers as Professors Agassiz, Guyon, and Rogers, would have been appreciated by popular audience.—But now they instruct and delight great multitudes.

In regard to Mr. Thoreau, we are glad to hear that he is about issuing a book, which will contain these lectures, and will enable us perhaps to judge better of their merit.[57]

Theodore Parker was a frequent lecturer at the Salem Lyceum although he did not deliver as many lectures as Emerson. The following is a list of the dates and titles of Parker's Salem lectures:

1844–1845	Roman Slavery
1845–1846	The Progress of Man
1848–1849	Transcendentalism
1849–1850	Educated Classes
1850–1851	The False and the True Idea of the Gentleman
1853–1854	The Function of the Beautiful in Human Development
1854–1855	The Anglo Saxon
	The Condition, Character, and Prospects of America

1855–1856   Relation of Productive Industry to Social Progress
1856–1857   Benjamin Franklin
1857–1858   Opportunities of Americans for Aiding Human Progress[58]

On Wednesday evening January 10, 1849, Parker delivered his "Transcendentalism" lecture before the Salem Lyceum.[59] The lecture, a clear and comprehensive discussion of the movement, reviews the history of the philosophic attitudes toward epistemology in order to set the stage for the emergence of the new philosophy. Parker discussed inductive and deductive reasoning, a priori knowledge, intuition, and sensation. He then went on to discuss the importance of Transcendentalism for physics, politics, ethics, and religion. In physics, he cites the example of the whole being greater than a part; in politics, he says: "By birth man is a citizen of the universe, subject to God; no oath of allegiance, no king, no parliament, no congress, no people, can absolve him from his natural fealty thereto, and alienate a man born to the rights, born to the duties, of a citizen of God's universe";[60] "In morals," he says "conscience is complete and reliable as the eye for colors, the ear for sounds, the touch and taste for their purposes. While experience shows what has been or is, conscience shows what should be and shall";[61] in religion, he says: "Transcendentalism admits a religious faculty, element, or nature in man, as it admits a moral, intellectual, and sensational faculty,—that man by nature is a religious being as well as moral, intellectual, sensational. . . ."[62] Parker's summary, while not innovative, is incisive and firm in tone. Here is a portion of that summary: "The problem of transcendental philosophy is no less than this, to revise the experience of mankind and try its teachings by the nature of mankind; to test ethics by conscience, science by reason; to try the creeds of the churches, the constitutions of the states by the constitution of the universe; to reverse what is wrong, supply what is wanting, and command the just."[63]

The reviewer of Mr. Parker's lecture in the Salem *Observer* indicated an awareness of the difficulties of a lecture on Transcendentalism but stated that Mr. Parker amply overcame those difficulties and did so before a sizable audience. The following is the *Observer*'s review in its entirety:

Theodore Parker on Transcendentalism

A very full audience assembled on Wednesday evening, to hear the Rev. Theodore Parker discourse on *Transcendentalism.*—He gave their ideas an airing in the region of metaphysics, to which popular audiences are not often led, but he proved so good a guide, indicated the path so clearly and simply, and placed each foot down so firmly, that probably few regretted the ascent of the mount of vision up which they climbed. Not least amongst Mr. Parker's excellencies as a writer, is the facility with which he simplifies difficult subjects, picking the bones of technicality out of a theme, and making it quite easy of digestion.

Mr. Parker premised that there were two great philosophical systems, the Inductive and the Deductive;—the former, that which observes particular phenomena or facts of experience, and draws therefrom great and general conclusions; the latter, that which presumes certain great facts or principles to be correct, and deduces all minor details from them. These two methods he illustrated at some length.

He then divided philosophical enquirers into two schools, the Sensational and the Transcendental. The former holds that all knowledge, all thoughts, notions, ideas, enter the mind through the senses; that there can be no conception in the intellect which has not been previously in some one or all of the senses. The Transcendentalist holds that there are thoughts and ideas in the mind which transcend the senses, which do not come from them or through them, which are originally ingrained in the mind, and which come by intuition.

Mr. Parker then proceeded to test the two schools by their fruits. He looked at their results in the several fields of physics, politics, ethics, and theology. In this examination he dwelt principally upon the Sensational philosophers, and a pretty bad character he gave them. He gave their conclusions as, in physics, uncertainty; in politics, that might makes right; that the power of the king in monarchies, or of the majority in republics, is the only test of right; in ethics compromise and expediency; in theology, doubt and uncertainty, a finite and imperfect God. Hobbes, Hume, Priestly, Berkely, Paley, he regarded as the truest disciples of the different branches of the sensational school, which might also be termed the English school. The first French Revolution he regarded as a legitimate result of that philosophy and a true exponent of its principles.

In reviewing the Transcendentalist, Mr. Parker was less thorough, and, regarding them with greater favor, his remarks were eulogistic and extremely fine. His enumeration of the Absolute truths of Transcendental ethics was most eloquent. Transcendentalism he drew as being one with pure Christianity, and Jesus of Nazareth he claimed as the only exemplar of its truths the world has yet seen. The Declaration of Independence he instanced as a fruit of transcendental politics.

Sensationalism he regarded as dependent upon human history; Transcendentalism upon human nature. He asked if this system of Absolute truth would ever prevail in the world; and human history says No! but human nature says yes! [64]

In addition to these lectures by Emerson, Thoreau, and Parker, the Salem Lyceum offered other lectures that although not purely Transcendental or on Transcendentalism itself, were, nevertheless, on subjects or figures that were related to Transcendental interests. Some of these lectures were the following:

Year	Lecturer	Title
1837–1838	Jones Very	Epic Poetry
1843–1844	E. P. Whipple	The Leading Poets as Wordsworth, Byron, Shelley, etc.
1844–1845	Orestes Brownson	Social Reform

Emerson
P48
52

Walker
54
57
p58 tenets !

1846–1847	David Barlow	Swedenborg
1850–1851	T. W. Higginson	Man and Nature
	Sylvester Judd, Jr.	Origin of the Human Language
1851–1852	George Briggs	George Fox
	T. W. Higginson	Mahommed
	Sylvester Judd, Jr.	Use of the Beautiful [65]

Amos Bronson Alcott also gave at least one of his "conversations" in Salem but the date of that event is not available. Sophia Hawthorne gave the following account of the evening's entertainment as well as her impressions of Mr. Alcott in a fragment of a letter published by her daughter:

"My husband bought a ticket for himself, and went with me!! Mr. Alcott spent an evening with us a week or more ago, and was very interesting; telling, at my request, about his youth, and peddling, etc. There were six ladies and six gentlemen present last Monday evening. They assembled at Mr. Stone's. Miss Hannah Hodges, Mrs. J. C. Lee, and two ladies whom I did not know, besides Mrs. Stone and myself; Mr. Frothingham, Mr. William Silsbee, Mr. Shackford, of Lynn, Mr. Pike, Mr. Streeter, and my husband besides Mr. Stone and his son. Mr. Alcott said he would commence with the Nativity, and first read Milton's Hymn. Then he retreated to his corner, and for about an hour and three quarters kept an even flow of thought, without a word being uttered by any other person present. Then Mr. Stone questioned him upon his use of the word 'artistic;' which provoked a fine analysis from him of the word 'artist' as distinguished from 'artisan.' I thought the whole monologue very beautiful and clear." [66]

Octavius B. Frothingham gives another account of Alcott's appearance in Salem: "I remember, in connection with Samuel Johnson, collecting an audience for Mr. A. B. Alcott the most adroit soliloquizer I ever listened to, who delivered in a vestry-room a series of those remarkable 'conversations'—versations with the *con* left out—for which he was celebrated. It was, in many respects, a happy time."[67]

There can be no doubt that the Salem Lyceum was extremely effective in promoting the cause of Transcendentalism in Salem. It brought before large and interested audiences the movement's brightest stars, men who in the inseparability of their unique personalities and philosophies, presented more than a mere accounting of their beliefs. Emerson, of necessity, spoke of the practical aspects of Transcendentalism but it was that very necessity that helped to popularize Transcendental beliefs. The lyceum allowed speakers to test their ideas, immediately assess audience reactions to them, and to revise those ideas, if necessary, prior to their publication. Emerson once remarked that he often tried his lectures out on small lyceums, and after a number of readings finally polished the lectures enough to deliver them in the city. "Poor men," Emerson said, "they little know how different that lecture will be when it is given in New York, or is printed."[68] Nor was Emerson unique in this respect. Thoreau's work had similarly benefited from lyceum readings. Salem was not the only place where he read parts of *Walden.* He drew from that work ten or more times (as compared to *A Week on the Concord and Merrimack Rivers* on which he drew only once), and there can be little doubt that each public reading helped Thoreau to improve the work. Although Henry Seidel Canby had stated that "nearly everything Thoreau wrote was originally conceived as a lecture," not until the publication of Walter Harding's biography of Thoreau was the importance of the lyceum for Thoreau appreciated or treated with any degree of thoroughness.[69]

The lectures on Transcendentalism by Parker and Walker attest to the interest in the new philosophy. The fact that Salem Lyceum members chose these men, both of whom were eminently qualified to speak on the subject, was fortunate. They presented objective, philosophically sound, and interesting lectures that sought more to heighten appreciation of what the movement had to offer than to simplify or popularize. The minor figures in the Transcendental movement lectured on subjects that were either significant influences on the precepts of the movement as a whole or were yet more specialized and diversified aspects of Transcendentalism. They all helped to fill out the total picture. Indeed, it is difficult to think of men or lectures that the people of Salem would have needed to provide a more comprehensive picture of Transcendentalism.

In addition to the lyceum, the spirit of Transcendentalism entered Salem in many and diverse ways. Those Transcendentalists who spoke before the lyceum were often authors as well, and the sale of their works was aided by their lyceum appearances. The lyceum was, in effect, an early form of advertisement in addition to its more obvious functions; it might even be considered a prototype of the "talk-show" publicity so common today in promoting books. People were, at least, more apt to remember the name of an author if he had appeared before their lyceum and consequently would be more likely to buy his work. The converse is also true: book buyers attended lectures by their favorite authors. Some book buyers, undoubtedly, thought they were buying what they had heard read before the lyceum and were surprised often to find otherwise. Some were interested in buying another work by the author they had heard in person. The quick sale of five hundred copies of *Nature* that took place within the first month after its publication was just as surprising to Emerson as it was to others.[70] Many people must have known that the book was forthcoming and, despite its complexity and anonymous authorship, purchased it.

No records are available on the sale of Transcendental works in Salem bookstores. These bookstores, however, kept up with the latest developments and advertised those works that were written by foreign authors in particular. Magazines and periodicals were advertised in both the *Gazette* and the *Observer*. Some of those were the *Christian Examiner* (liberal Unitarian publication edited by James Walker for a time),

The Knickerbocker (which was especially critical of Transcendentalism), *The New Englander*, the *North American Review*, the *Massachusetts Quarterly Review*, *Brownson's Quarterly Review*, and the *Boston Quarterly Review*, as well as excerpts, published in the local newspapers, of articles in other periodicals. These newspapers often published a short table of contents for periodicals that were newly published and occasionally did reviews of the entire contents, article by article, of a periodical. These reviews sometimes included excerpts of articles as well. The Salem *Gazette* for January 27, 1844, reviewed a recent number of *Brownson's Quarterly Review* and devoted most of the article to Brownson's thoughts on the church and his philosophic change of direction. The *Gazette* on January 9, 1846, not only published a review, reprinted from the *North American Review*, of Sylvester Judd's Transcendental novel *Margaret* but excerpts from the book as well. In a notice advertising the *Massachusetts Quarterly Review*, the Salem *Observer* commented on the second article in the number, "Swedenborg as a Theologian": "[it] contains valuable thoughts for those interested in the writings of this Swedish Seer—an increasing class we believe, including many who do not fully accept his annunciations, but are attracted to the study of his views, by their spiritual and sublime character, and purifying and elevating influence."[71] Such reviews, in short, helped the citizens of Salem to keep in touch with the latest activities of the Transcendentalists.

The local newspapers, the *Gazette* and the *Observer* chiefly, did other services, perhaps not intentionally, for the cause of Transcendentalism. On January 31, 1840, the *Gazette* published a short sketch of Swedenborg's life. Later, on November 14, 1846, the *Observer* reviewed a lecture on Swedenborg delivered by Rev. David H. Barlow in which Barlow connected Swedenborg to Fourier and talked about the meaning of correspondences: "Every material object stands for a spiritual fact.—Light, in the material world, corresponds to God's wisdom or truth; water corresponds to truth in a limited degree; heat and magnetism, are representative of love." On February 17, 1840, the *Gazette* published a short article on George Fox and the Quakers. The Quakers were a source of interest for the Salemites because the Quakers had been persecuted early in the town's history. Fox, however, has a certain degree of interest for a study of Transcendentalism in Salem because he had an influence on Emerson and because some of his beliefs had an influence on Transcendentalism. Fox was against institutionalized religion and spoke of Light (spirit, conscience) as a democratizing principle, very much as Emerson had done in his lecture "Water." In his Salem lecture on Fox, Emerson indicated the relationship of Fox's thinking to Transcendental thought: "It is, I think, the most remarkable fact in the history of the Quakers that the books and tracts written to announce and defend their faith are a string of citations from all the sages, such as one would expect to find in the lecture of Kant or Fichte on the Transcendental Philosophy. This extends even to the more abstruse questions which are commonly thought to be out of the domain of exact science and left to theorists called visionary, to Shelling, Novalis, and Swedenborg: the nature of animals, of dreams, of names."[72]

These were some of the ways that Transcendentalism entered Salem and came to be known by Salemites. But what of a native Transcendentalism? For that we must look more closely at Elizabeth Palmer Peabody and Jones Very, their lives and their philosophies.

Elizabeth Palmer Peabody's lifetime spanned nearly the entire nineteenth century.[73] She was born in Billerica, Massachusetts, in 1804 and died in Boston in 1894. Although she did not spend her entire life in Salem, she did live a considerable portion of it there and her strongest ties were to that town. Even in her long lifetime, the list of activities and accomplishments of this most energetic woman is staggering. She was a governess, a teacher, a student of Dr. Channing's, an assistant to Bronson Alcott in the famous Temple School (1835–37), and the author of *Record of a School: Exemplifying the General Principles of Spiritual Culture* (1835) and *Record of Conversations on the Gospels Held in Mr. Alcott's School* (1836–37), accounts of both their teaching methods. Her experiences in the schools molded her own ideas and prepared her for the promotion of the kindergarten movement in this country. Beginning in 1833 Elizabeth gave what she called "Conversations" for women that were similar in approach and purpose to the "Conversations" of Margaret Fuller and Bronson Alcott. Such conferences were seminars for which people paid a fee to converse with the teacher or celebrity for the purpose of personal enlightenment. In addition to these activities, Miss Peabody operated a bookstore in Boston that was a favorite meeting place for intellectuals, particularly the Transcendentalists. Along with good conversation, she provided her customers with foreign publications not readily available in this country, again a vital service especially for the eclectic Transcendentalists.

There was another side of Elizabeth Peabody, a side that is more interesting for our purposes. She was a Transcendentalist and her idealism and aesthetic sensibility, concerns that might have gone unnoticed in another age, fit in well with the movement that she in turn helped to form. She was a tremendously enthusiastic individual, but she balanced her enthusiasm by an unwillingness to be unduly optimistic. She was exceedingly well read, and in an age when the education of women was thought to be of dubious value at best, she was an intellectual on a par with all the leading figures in the movement. She knew Greek and Latin as well as some French and Hebrew. Her first Greek tutor was none other than Ralph Waldo Emerson, who told her at their first meeting that she already knew Greek and that there was little else he could teach her. They remained close friends from that time onward.[74] In her letters to Emerson and other important figures of the period Elizabeth plumbs the depths of the Tran-

scendental movement, discusses the most essential and profound philosophic questions with great clarity, and continually assesses the thoughts and beliefs of her contemporaries.
Her letters reveal her to be a direct, analytical, and trenchant
thinker.

Elizabeth Peabody's lifework was education. Louise Hall
Tharp comments on her as a teacher: "Her reputation as
an unusually gifted teacher was very clearly established,
for she was able to communicate to her pupils some of her
own passion for acquiring knowledge. There were those who
said that she lacked system and was too little of a drillmaster,
but no one ever failed to add that she was always inspira-
tional."[75] Elizabeth showed a great reverence for self-reliance
and independence, which she tried to foster in her students.
She had no formal schooling, came to her task without pre-
conceptions, and sought to apply any means necessary for
the accomplishment of her purposes. She worked so closely
with Bronson Alcott in the classroom and on the books that
grew from their experiences that their educational attitudes
were very similar. Elizabeth agreed with the main tenet of
Alcott's philosophy of education that children should first
be taught to know themselves and that the teacher should
be an expert in then drawing out what the children intui-
tively knew. Emerson had also said that "education is the
drawing out the Soul,"[76] indicating a commonality of belief
that reflects more a particular view of life and the world
than any personal influences among these three thinkers.
Along with the encouragement of self-reliance, Elizabeth
relied heavily on her own intuition in the classroom and tried
to encourage such intuition as well as introspection and moral
values in her students. It was, however, on the matter of moral
values that Elizabeth and Alcott disagreed and parted company. She had always felt that Alcott went too far with his
teaching of self-reliance and produced, she believed, a kind
of egotistical outlook in students. When Alcott's *Conversations on the Gospels* was about to appear, she feared attacks

from the Unitarians. Her assumption was correct; fortunately, she had separated from Alcott and was not the subject of these attacks. She later retreated from such great emphasis on introspection and moved philosophically toward a belief in the teaching of the physical activities of children. This finally led to her work with Friedrich Froebel in Germany and the founding of the kindergarten movement in America. In her new concern with handicrafts and physical activities she calls forth a natural comparison to Maria Montessori, the twentieth-century Italian educator who was responsible for the establishment of Montessori schools all over the world. [77]

Elizabeth Peabody was a catalytic agent for the Transcendental movement. She delighted in introducing her acquaintances to one another because she thought, in most cases, that they ought to know each other, and in this respect her actions were always a bit too contrived and obvious. Yet, it is precisely such a personality that was so necessary for this particular movement in which so many often insular but nevertheless like-minded people needed to talk and to encourage one another. Among her greatest "triumphs" were the discovery of Jones Very and the early encouragement of Nathaniel Hawthorne as a writer shortly after his period of isolation in Salem. Elizabeth liked to be in control, to guide, and to advise, and in this regard she became for Hawthorne, at least, a little overbearing at times. [78] Her aggressiveness, incisiveness, and immense learning must have put him off balance at times.

Elizabeth discovered Jones Very when he delivered his lecture "Epic Poetry" at the Salem Lyceum in 1837. [79] She had just returned to Salem from Boston after an absence of several years while she served as Alcott's assistant in the Temple School. She had heard that an interesting neighbor of hers was to lecture before the Salem Lyceum and so she went to the lecture hall accompanied by her father. She was somewhat skeptical and not as enthusiastic as she ordinarily might have been. Hawthorne had paid a visit to her house six weeks earlier and the excitement of that particular encounter still stirred her blood. Perhaps subconsciously she did not wish to make another "discovery" until the enigma of Hawthorne had been clarified.

Elizabeth sat in the front row of the Lyceum Hall and watched the young Harvard Divinity School student as he nervously awaited his audience. Once the lecture had started, she thought that Very exhibited a strange combination of nervousness and confidence. More interestingly for her, he seemed aloof. Very's lecture was authoritative, accurate, and sincere, she thought, but she was not thoroughly convinced that she wanted to become involved with yet another young "genius":

> When the lecture was finished Very "stood for a moment— uncertain, shy, and embarrassed." Elizabeth suddenly rose from her seat and before she realized what she was saying, she had asked him to go home with her. He grasped her outstretched hand "like a drowning man a straw," and gratefully accepted the invitation. As she walked with him she expressed her "delight" in the lecture and her desire "to hear his thought on all the current subjects of the day, which were mainly the transcendental topics." She was pleased but not surprised to find "he was an enthusiastic listener to Mr. Emerson," and he told her "he was writing on Shakespeare, who had, he thought, betrayed his individual spiritual experience in Hamlet." From the beginning Elizabeth was struck by the intensity of his conversation, especially later that evening when he explained his theory that Shakespeare's genius was imperfect because it was incomplete.[80]

The Salem lecture changed Very's life significantly. He had met Elizabeth Peabody and she would open many doors for the young intellectual. He had no sooner left the Peabody house when Elizabeth wrote to Emerson about their meeting. She urged Emerson to invite Very to lecture in Concord and to talk to him.[81] Later, Very was to meet not only Emerson but also William Ellery Channing, Bronson Alcott, and other members of the Transcendental Club.

Jones Very was born on August 28, 1813, in Salem and was named after his father, a sea captain. His mother Lydia Very was his father's first cousin and a remarkable woman by any standards.[82] She was liberal-minded, atheistic, and aggressive. She refused to make the usual contractual marriage agreement, thinking that such an arrangement was unnatural. She had a different idea; she preferred to believe that marriage was based on love. Despite her insistence on principle and her seeming aloofness, she was affectionate and extremely devoted to her children; consequently, she was not eager to have her husband take young Jones to sea, as was customary in those days.

When he was nine years old, Jones Very was nevertheless taken by his father on a voyage to Kronstadt, the port city of St. Petersburg. He acted as a cabin boy on this voyage, a trip which lasted approximately seven months. Two other voyages took the boy to England, France, Portugal, and New Orleans where he attended school during the winter term of 1823–24.[83] His father became sick on his final voyage home and died soon after reaching Salem. Captain Very's will prompted a lawsuit against Lydia, which she won. She was thus able to buy a modest house on Federal Street where the family remained until Lydia Louisa Ann, Jones Very's youngest sister and the last member of the family, died in 1901 and where the poet himself died in 1880 after living for years in relative seclusion.[84]

Nature was very important to young Jones Very. His mother was the envy of all Salem for the plants she cultivated, and the boy grew up in a home brightened by colorful plants the year round. As he grew older, he showed his love of nature in the long walks he took in and around Salem. A contemplative boy and a good student, at the age of thirteen he was given the task of providing for the Very family, a responsibility he carried on for the next eight years. He worked in a Salem auction room as a helper and become interested in the books he handled, particularly the volumes of poetry. Lydia Very had been a writer of poetry; this influence as well as his reading and the guidance of his early tutors, J. Worcester Fox and Henry K. Oliver, fostered Very's own interest in poetry.[85] Oliver also aided Very immeasurably in the pursuit of his career. Oliver advised Very to keep a journal, to make a list of books he read and liked, and to take from those books passages he admired for a commonplace book. The first of three notebooks that Very kept "shows unmistakable signs of Oliver's attempt to help his protégé free himself from the intellectual and emotional domination of Lydia Very."[86] It seems clear that Oliver wished to rid Very of the influence of the apparent materialism and atheism of his mother.

Jones Very's first poem to appear in print, "Original Poetry for the Salem Observer," appeared in the *Observer* on August 10, 1833. Three days later Very wrote a forty-line poem in heroic couplets protesting slavery; he had observed the treatment of the slaves and Indians of Louisiana during his stay there in 1823–24. Very's sympathy with the slaves is in the mainstream of romantic literature and many lines of the poem are reminiscent of Goldsmith, Crabbe, and Cowper.[87] Much of Very's poetry is uneven. For Emerson, at least, this was to Very's credit for as Emerson said in his 1840 *Dial* article on contemporary poetry, true genius is most likely incompatible with brilliance of technique and form.[88]

Very served Oliver as an assistant in the Latin School and thereby gained the advanced standing of a second term sophomore when he enrolled in Harvard in February of 1834. As was his experience in learning to write, college was an important change in the direction of Very's life and one that was significant in terms of his family history. He had broken the strong ties that had wedded his family to the sea.

During his Harvard years, Very continued to be a serious student despite his involvement in the famous Dunkin Rebellion soon after his arrival at the college.[89] Very had worked for a long while, was older than most of the other students, and enjoyed his studies. Ancient and modern literature were popular subjects with him, but his main interest was religion, a strange preference considering the attitudes and practices of his mother.

During his senior year, eight of Very's poems appeared in *Harvardiana,* a student literary magazine. By this time he had also sent a number of poems to the Salem *Observer* and he had won the Bowdoin Prize an unprecedented second time for his essays.[90] Upon his graduation on August 31, 1836, Very finished second in his class and was appointed freshman tutor in Greek on the basis of his undergraduate record in that subject.[91]

In September 1838, at the start of his second year as Greek tutor, Very had in his class Samuel Johnson, Jr., a young Salemite and the son of a prominent Salem physician. Johnson would one day tour Europe with Very's brother and would also become the greatest Orientalist of his time in America. Johnson was a minor Transcendentalist and a good friend of another peripheral Salem Transcendentalist and chronicler of the movement, Octavius B. Frothingham, who wrote an extended essay entitled "Transcendentalism." Frothingham, a Unitarian minister, spent nine important and impressionable years (1847–55), beginning when he was twenty-five years old, in the pastorate of the North Church in Salem and later wrote *Transcendentalism in New England: A History* (1876), perhaps the best history by a contemporary of the movement.

In that same September, Very had begun to show signs of religious fanaticism. He announced the second coming of Christ, and then actually saw himself as a second Christ. During his earlier Harvard years, he gradually became caught up in a Transcendentalism that was more mystical and religious than would have seemed comfortable for most other Transcendentalists. His early reading of the Scottish philosophers, his contacts with George Ticknor at Harvard, and his interest in Shakespeare and sonneteering all shaped his philosophic outlook. The elder Samuel Johnson had heard rumors about

Very and wrote to his son to determine whether or not he had been affected by him. The young Johnson had noted Very's peculiar manner and he wrote to his father to assure him that everything was quite all right. Young Johnson wrote that Very "carried his reasoning farther and deeper into subjects on which he spoke, than the extent to which [he had] been accustomed to hear them urged."[92] No sooner had Johnson posted his letter than Jones Very entered his classroom and began speaking irrationally and fanatically. Having crossed the line into temporary insanity, Very was relieved of his teaching duties by Harvard officials on September 13, 1838.[93] Very was sent home to Salem to rest; shortly thereafter he was sent to McLean Hospital for one month after which he returned to Salem.[94] He never returned to his Harvard teaching position.

The attempt to define Very's Transcendentalism, if indeed he may be classified a Transcendentalist, is, of course, not easy.[95] In a recent study, Nathan Lyons has written that Very has been "wrongly catalogued" with the Transcendentalists.[96] Very did, however, attend the "Hedge Club" meetings, and he was associated with the Peabodys, Bronson Alcott, Cyrus Bartol, James Freeman Clarke, and Emerson. Very did attend Margaret Fuller's "Conversations" and Emerson's lectures. His friendship and later quarrels with Emerson and the contrast between the philosophies of the two men perhaps offer the best insights into Very's position vis-à-vis Transcendentalism.

The major points of comparison between Very and Emerson are their attitudes toward Nature, God, man, and self. For Emerson everything is secondary to Nature; for Very all things are secondary to God. Emerson seeks to find self through subservience to Nature and Very seeks God by abandoning self. Emerson wished man to be a "transparent eyeball," to be a seer of the richness and complexity of the world even if that meant reflecting its inconsistencies and paradoxes as well. Emerson's God was Nature and it was an impersonal

God. Very was sure of his God—sure that He existed and sure that He was immanent. Indeed, so fervent was he in that belief that he actually identified with God. Emerson's view was comprehensive and encompassing; Very's outlook was not as expansive, but was singular and Christian, and for those reasons, he thought, ultimately large. Emerson was delighted by complexity and organicism, whereas Very sought to clarify complexity by aligning himself with his God in a somewhat more static relationship. That these men sought a higher reality and that they believed they must give themselves over to that reality through some form of transcendence makes them like-minded, but insofar as they felt differently about the intermediaries in that process, they are very far apart philosophically.

Qualification and caution are necessary in discussing the Transcendentalism of Elizabeth Palmer Peabody and Jones Very, yet it must be emphasized that they were unmistakably a part of the movement and showed philosophical affinities for it. Perhaps the point to remember here, though, is not that Very and Peabody were narrow enough in their thinking to be a part of the movement proper but that the movement was generous enough to encompass them. Beyond this, however, these two figures serve to show both the influence of external Transcendental forces—Emerson, Thoreau, Parker, and Walker—and the rise of a native Transcendentalism. Salem sought out the new thinkers of the age through its lyceum at the same time that it made its own contributions to the movement in such native talents as Elizabeth Peabody, Jones Very, William Silsbee, and, later, Octavius B. Frothingham and Samuel Johnson, Jr. And, of course, there was Nathaniel Hawthorne. But before turning to that most famous of all Salemites, a writer who was not only fascinated by but critical of the new spirit that had come upon the land, it will be useful to describe and assess Salem's general reaction to this new literary and philosophical movement.

SALEM'S REACTION TO
TRANSCENDENTALISM

S ALEM'S reaction to Transcendentalism was similar to the
reaction to the movement in New England and the rest
of the country.[1] With the exception of the miracles question,
a theological dispute of questionable impact on the average
churchgoer, there was no united counterreaction against
Transcendentalism because the invader, more felt than seen,
was shadowy in itself. Reaction there was nevertheless, but
it is doubtful that it ever reached the proportions of resistance.
This counterinfluence, although more personal and subtle,
never lessened the inquisitive ardor of Salemites or the spirit
of free inquiry that had come to characterize Salem. Because
there were important personalities in the town, who sometimes appeared larger than the issues involved, people and
their views became inseparable and argument always ran
the risk of becoming *ad hominem* in character. Fear of personal attacks and an inability to grasp basic issues, on the
other hand, made other criticisms of Transcendentalism more
oblique and general. This chapter first examines the varied
brief criticisms found mostly in Salem's newspapers and then
concentrates on the more involved personal relationships of
key figures.

On March 21, 1834, the Salem *Gazette* published a short
article that discussed the worth of the lectures given at the
lyceum. The article referred to the sizable number of people
who had attended the lectures but generally withheld any
real praise. Part of that article read as follows: "Whether

much information is imparted by this promiscuous mode of lecturing or whether some other better plan can be devised for diffusing knowledge amongst the people, are questions which we do not pretend to decide. . . ." The remark that the writer will not "pretend to decide" the worth of the lecturing system is gratuitous since the question has already been raised, however indirectly, by that remark. The misgiving on the part of the writer may very well have had to do with the rather unorthodox mixture of entertainment and learning that the lyceum offered. Indeed, one lyceum-goer suggested that some provision ought to be made to channel into some form of higher education the enthusiasm for knowledge that was created at the lyceum. The comment seems to forecast a trend that was clearly seen and could be shown more forcibly some years later. The following article appeared in the *Observer* on November 3, 1855:

LECTURING. The thing is being overdone all together. Of lecturing latterly there is no end. Courses succeed courses, like discharges of verbal musketry, while single and special addresses are successively let off like the occasional shots of sportsmen afield. The people are lectured to their heart's content, listening like the good patient public that they are, to whatever any body has to say upon whatever subject.—The lecturer is abroad—and the people are abroad also, for there is no staying at home when so frequent calls are made upon one's time at the lecture room. The reading of books for ends of practical usefulness, for the attainment of knowledge, bids fair to become so old fashioned as to be quite out of date, since the voluble gentlemen who occupy the lecturers' desks dispense all knowledge upon all subjects, ready prepared, digested and perfected. In this short way the public can be told all they want to know, without the toil and trouble of reading, study, and investigation for themselves.

Never before did lecturing rage as it threatens to during the coming season, and if the community is not vastly wiser and better next spring it will be because there is not always so much value in "words, words, words" as we sometimes think there is. The human tongue is a useful member and the human ear is a valuable arrangement. But both must harmonize and work together. The tongue should entertain a due respect for the rights of the ears. Silence is a privilege which the latter are entitled occasionally to enjoy. The demand to "lend me your ears" is one which public talkers ought to make with modesty, and certainly not to insist upon being granted every day of the seven.

The writer's objections here seem to reside with the lecture-goer and not with the lecturer himself. If the lecture material presented was made digestible that was part of the lecturer's task, and if the lecture-goer did not question what was being said it can hardly be considered a fault of the lecturing system. Finally, the frequency of the lectures themselves was determined by public demand; if attendance had fallen off, there would have been fewer lectures.

The major criticism that recurs throughout the reviews of Emerson's lectures in particular, and one criticism that was later leveled against Transcendentalism in general, was the claim that the Transcendental lectures were unnecessarily vague or, worse yet, incomprehensible. Almost every reviewer of Emerson's lectures, wherever he lectured, laments that an accurate paraphrase or even a summary is virtually impossible given the speaker's unusual style. Indeed, Emerson himself wished that there be no summaries of his lectures published in the newspapers. He wrote the following indignant letter to the editor of the *Commonwealth* on January 7, 1852:

Dear Sir,

I am exceedingly vexed by finding in your paper, this morning, precisely such a report of one of my lectures, as I wrote to you a fortnight since to entreat you to defend me from. I wrote, at the same time, to the other newspapers, & they have all kindly respected my request, & abstained. My lectures are written to be read as lectures in different places, & then to be reported by myself. Tomorrow, I was to have read this very lecture in Salem, & your reporter does all he can to kill the thing to every hearer, by putting him in possession beforehand of the words of each statement that struck him, as nearly as he could copy them. Abuse me, & welcome, but do not transcribe me. Now that your reporter has broken the line, I cannot expect the Traveller, & other journals to respect it, for it is a thing of concert. Defend me, another time.

> Respectfully,
> R. W. Emerson[2]

Emerson's style was, of course, part of his message rather than an act of conscious obfuscation to avoid paraphrase. He shows very early in his writings his awareness that rhetoric is both a product of and an influence upon one's perceptual mode—that new perceptions are communicated best by an original rhetoric. The Transcendental style was well known and the word *Transcendental* became synonymous with *unintelligible* or *incomprehensible*. The writer of the following article, which appeared in the Salem *Observer* on April 17, 1841, apparently found a passage of meaningless prose and jokingly sought to show it as the origin of the Transcendental style and that the Transcendentalists were, in fact, not very original in their rhetoric, as many must have thought they were.

Origin of Transcendentalism

We think we have traced the origin of transcendentalism in the Chaldean Oracles. A collection of them was first given to the public by Taylor, the English translator of the works of Plato. We cannot in the space of a short paragraph afford any thing like an exposition of these Oracles. Let a short quotation from them suffice; as it will show conclusively that the peculiar style of the modern transcendentalists is not *original*. Read the following paragraph from the Chaldean Oracles by Theargists:

"It is not proper to understand that intelligible with

vehemence but with the extended flame of an extended intellect; a flame which measures all things except that intelligible. But it is requisite to understand this. For if you incline your mind, you will understand it, though not vehemently. It becomes you, therefore, bring with you the pure convertible eye of your soul, to entend the void intellect to the intelligible, that you may learn its nature, because it has a subsistence above intellect."

Concerning the energy of this intellect about the intelligible, it is remarked: Eagerly urging itself toward the centre of resounding light.

Another parody, which appeared in the Salem *Observer* on May 27, 1843, was critical of Transcendentalism and, more particularly, of Emerson:

Transcendentalism. This *ism*, the bantling of German philosophy, and the foster child of Carlyle and Emerson, is thus "hit off" in a late number of the Southern Rose.

"Ralph Waldo Emerson is like unto a man who saith unto all the children and dear middle aged people of his neighborhood, "O come, let us go yonder and dance a beautiful dance at the foot of the rainbow. There will be treasures beneath our feet, and drops of all colors over our heads: and we shall be in the very presence of the mysteries of nature. And we and the rainbow shall be one—and the drops shall be usefulness—and the drops shall be righteousness and purity of heart—and mortality and immortality shall be identical—and sin and holiness—and labor and rest vulgarity and gentility—study and idleness—solitude and society, —black and white—shall all become one great commingled homogeneous and heterogeneous spot of pure glorification forever."

Then all the children and the dear middle aged people exclaimed, "beautiful, beautiful! Let us go yonder, and dance beneath the foot of the rainbow." And they all go forth with Emerson at their head and Carlyle in advance of him,—and Richter and Spinosa several rods in advance of Carlyle—and they seek the foot of the rainbow; but it recedes as they proceed. At length, wearied and scattered, they all returned to the humble village, and will be con-

tented with admiring the rainbow at a distance, and will
be greatful for the dark, colorless drops that come down
to refresh their heads, and will permit both rainbow and
drops to carry up their thoughts to the Mysterious Being
who created the whole, together with themselves—and so
continue to walk piously and practically to their graves."

Although it may be argued that the *Observer* was merely re-
porting what the *Southern Rose* had said about Emerson, the
use of *"ism"* in the introduction helps to establish the tone
and clarify the newspaper's attitude. The suffix "ism" was
used in a review, also critical of style, of Carlyle's *Past and
Present,* which appeared in the *Observer* on October 21, 1843:
"This is the hardest book to read that ever fell to our lot, except *Paradise Lost.* It abounds in gems of truth, expressed in
barbarous English, on which the Queen should at once place
an injunction. Its points are mainly local, and must be keen
felt at home where Chartism, Puseyism, and various other
isms are rife. Carlyle's peculiarities of style will procure him
many readers and some admirers." Interestingly the reviewer
suggests that "peculiarities of style" are only surface attrac-
tions that will not hold the attention of all readers. This certainly was not the case with Emerson as we shall see.

The following review, which appeared in the Salem
Observer on February 3, 1849, reprinted what must be one of
the most "glowing" descriptions of Emerson's lectures ever
recorded:

RALPH WALDO EMERSON. The Boston Post thus
speaks of one of Mr. Emerson's "lectures"; the brilliant
description is itself an exemplification of the thing described:
    "It is quite out of character to say Mr. Emerson lec-
tures—he does no such thing. He drops nectar—he chips
out sparks—he exhales odors—he lets off mental skyrockets
and fireworks—he spouts fire, and conjuror-like draws
ribbons out of his mouth. He smokes, he sparkles, he im-
provises, he shouts, he sings, he explodes like a bundle of

crackers, he goes off in fiery eruptions like a volcano, but he does not *lecture.* °°° He is a vitalized speculation—a talking essence—a sort of celestial emanation—a bit of transparency broken from the spheres—a spiritual prism through which we see all beautiful rays of immaterial existences. His leaping fancy mounts upward like an india rubberball, and drifts and falls like a snowflake or a feather. He moves in the region of similitudes. He comes through the air like a cherubim with a golden trumpet in his mouth, out of which he blows tropes and figures and gossamer transparencies of suggestive fancies. He takes high flights, and sustains himself without ruffling a feather. He inverts the rainbow and uses it for a swing—now sweeping the earth, and now clapping his hands among the stars."

It is obvious, however, that there is a satirical undertone in all this unbridled praise. The piece is double-edged as even the writer for the *Observer* wrote: "The brilliant description is itself an exemplification of the thing described."

An unpublished manuscript, dated November 2, 1846, of a lecture delivered in Salem gives the views of a foreign visitor on this matter of stylistics. Jonathan P. Nichols, Jr., a Scottish professor of astronomy at the University of Glasgow whose own effectiveness as a lecturer at the Salem Lyceum was publicly acclaimed in the Salem *Gazette* (January 14, 1848), points to an interesting and essentially paradoxical situation regarding Transcendental rhetoric on the lecture platform.

The object of the following remarks is, to present some thoughts upon that tendency to what is called Idealism, which seems so peculiarly characteristic of this age, and which (I believe) is so little understood, and so generally misapprehended; and to show, how the present endeavors of (so called) Transcendental Reformers, have in view, instead of an Ideal, a practical good. . . . One of the greatest obstacles (it is true) to the diffusion of this Idealism *is* the remoteness of the language in which modern reformers clothe their thoughts, when presenting this Idea to the public mind. To them who have beheld the exceeding beauty and likewise the vastness of the change which they so desire; there is almost a *necessity* to call forth the most high meaning and high sounding words, which deep thinkers have even invented to express deep thoughts; and the very gestures and actions of our reform lecturers seem straining higher & higher to grasp the sublimity, which they attempted to bring to the audience to whom they speak. It is not probable that this has the desired effect of imposing knowledge and exciting sympathy; but perhaps even to the contrary extreme perplexes and darkens the minds, it would enlighten. How then will men of low degree learn from these high set Idealists what they mean when they can not rise to the comprehension of the words in which this mystic revelation is hid (and not unfolded) if the expounder can not stoop to the A.B.C. of language and express it?[3]

The lyceum's seventeenth and eighteenth courses (1845–47) offered the year before and the year after the date of this manuscript included in both cases such speakers as W. H. Channing, Theodore Parker, R. W. Emerson, T. T. Stone, a young Unitarian minister of Transcendental inclinations, and Samuel Johnson, Jr., and provided Nichols with the opportunity to hear firsthand some of the most eloquent speakers in the Transcendental movement.

Nichols and the Transcendentalists must have been trying to accomplish different ends. Nichols' task was undoubtedly to clarify in an interesting way scientific technicalities—to explain a pre-existing system. The Transcendentalists, on the other hand, set themselves the task of explaining a system that, although known to themselves, was only dimly perceived, if perceived at all, by lecture-goers. In a sense then, to put the solution in McLuhan's terms, the medium was the message. To separate rhetoric and message was understandably impossible; to accept or to reject the rhetoric of the movement was to accept or to reject the subject of it—Transcendentalism itself.

This is the extent of the short criticisms found in the Salem newspapers. At a later date, in 1878, Henry K. Oliver took a longer view and offered a more informed and, therefore, more accurate account of Emerson's influence on Salem:

> For variety in subject, aptness in treatment, great intellectual display, and profound power of thought, I can imagine nothing superior. It used to be said of him that he was too much of a transcendentalist, prone to discuss subjects transcending the reach of the senses, and so beyond reach of the average comprehension. Of his ability to grapple and to vanquish each and all of those he attempted, there is no lack of proof, while the very fact of his frequent appearance here, shows conclusively that he was never beyond our reach, however high he soared, and that is a compliment to us, and we were never willing to dispense with his teachings. Not seldom were we startled by some new application of an old word to a new use, or of an old word applied felicitously to a new thought, and clothing that thought with new attraction. His lectures that I specially mention, were those on Manners, and on Napoleon, and most impressive and winning of attention were they. To measure them all aright, one would need to be Emerson himself, and I will only venture a word or two about these two. He gave his own conception of fine manners. One meets them, he said, but once or twice in one's whole life. Their charm is that they are not assumed, neither factitious nor fictitious, being of very nature, natural. Concealing nothing, they display their perfectness by their naturalness, illustrated in each act and word—their beautiful nature being more beautiful than any beautiful form or face, this unartful art of good manners being the very finest of the fine arts. Are we now, in family and school and daily life, allowing it to become one of the lost arts?. . .
>
> Mr. Emerson's manner and pose of body on the stage, seemed, at first sight, to have an element of formality, something of stately dignity. Yet this impression vanished very soon, and the hearer was won by the look of a cheerful and cheering face, the sound of a firm, distinct, and mellifluous voice, and an outpour in the very best English of the most instructive and suggestive thought.[4]

Once again the rhetoric of the moment, this time specifically Emerson's own rhetoric, is called to our attention, but Oliver is quick to add that "he was never beyond our reach."

Information concerning Salem's attitude toward Haw-thorne's association with Brook Farm and reform in general is limited, but helpful. The Salem *Observer* announced on July 17, 1852, the publication of Hawthorne's *The Blithedale Romance*, but does not use the occasion to express any dis-satisfaction with Hawthorne's connection with Brook Farm:

THE BLITHEDALE ROMANCE. By Nathaniel Haw-thorne. Boston: Ticknor, Reed, & Fields, pp 228.

This is the title of Hawthorne's new romance announced some weeks since, and just published by Ticknor & Co. We presume the author's reputation is now so firmly estab-lished that the 'reading public,' or that part of them who can appreciate genius have been enjoying the anticipation of the Blithedale Romance, ever since its announcement. Our own expectations have been highly raised, and a very cursery view of the book (which we have not yet had time to read in the right mood) has only served to whet our appe-tite. It has been pronounced by competent critics, worthy of a higher rank than either "The Scarlet Letter," or "The House of Seven Gables." We think we give it as high praise as any book can deserve, in classing it equal to those books, and worthy to have been written by the author of them.

We have no intention of doing our readers the injustice of attempting anything like an analysis of the plot, or the character of the work. We are conscious that such informa-tion, even if skillfully done, would not be agreeable to our-selves, if we had the pleasure of reading it in contemplation. We therefore leave the book "without note or comment," merely giving an inkling of its contents from the preface, and heartily recommending it to all who like the "best works of the best authors."

The "Blithedale," described in this volume, the author confesses to be a "faint and not very faithful shadowing of Brook Farm, in Roxbury," an establishment formerly owned and occupied by a company of socialists, with whom Haw-thorne sojourned for a time. This general resemblance is carried out through the book, merely, as the author says, "to establish a theatre, a little removed from the highway of ordinary travel, where the creatures of his brain may play their phantasmagorical antics, without exposing them too close a comparison with the actual events of real lives;" and "without the slightest pretentions to illustrate a theory, or elicit a conclusion, favorable or otherwise, in respect to socialism." The characters are entirely fictitious, such, indeed, he says, as "might have been looked for at Brook Farm, but by some accident, never made their appearance there."

The Blithedale Romance may be found at the Bookstore of Henry Whipple & Son.

Several comments on reform appeared in Salem newspapers of the period, but it is difficult to tell just how representative these comments are of the town's overall response to this question. The first notice appeared in the Salem *Gazette* on January 20, 1843: "We would commend to those who blame the ministry for not entering more ernestly into the various phases of Social Reform, the following excellent remarks of the Rev. George Putnam, of Roxbury. They are worthy of being read and considered by every friend of the welfare and dignity of the Christian Church. 'Reform is good when it is based on Christian goodness. It's impossible without the church itself—Christianity itself.' "

A second, lengthier treatment of the subject appeared in the *Observer* on February 17, 1844:

SOCIALISM.

The advocates of Socialism have lately been making quite a stir in Boston. It seems, however, that they are divided into sects which do not harmonise in perfect brotherly love. At the head of that system which is called *Fourierism*, after the name of its founder, Charles Fourier, is Albert Brisbane of New York. Mr Brisbane, however, is a very dull speaker, and is not calculated to effect much for the cause by his eloquence. There are three Commu-

nities in this State established upon the Fourier plan,—one
in Milford, with Rev. Adin Ballon, at its head; another in
Roxbury, with Rev. Mr Ripley at its head; and another in
Northampton, Rev. Mr Adams at its head. We have not
heard that any one of these is in a very flourishing condition.
They recognise the right of individual property; and each
community is in fact a sort of corporation, the funds of
which are sold out in shares. This circumstance must of
course give rise to the same distinctions arising from differences of wealth, which are so much lamented in general
society. According to Mr Brisbane's plan, they have different priced tables, and those who enter the community,
without any property, are obliged to eat at the lowest
priced table! This seems to look rather aristocratic. We do
not undertake to say, however, that this idea of Brisbane's
is carried out in the Communities in this State.

The article concludes with a discussion of a socialistic community headed by John A. Collins at Skaneateles, New York,
and purports to show that this was at least one such community that seemed to be working. More interesting for our
purposes is the statement regarding Brisbane's dullness as a
speaker, which stands in such sharp contrast to comments on
Emerson's effectiveness as a speaker and thinker.

A third notice that appeared in the *Gazette* on November
23, 1847, cites Emerson: "Emerson says, very justly, that
society gains nothing, whilst a man, not himself renovated,
attempts to renovate things around him; he has become tedi-
ously good in some particular, but negligent or narrower
than the rest; and hypocrisy or vanity are often the disgust-
ing result." Interestingly, the attitude was one shared by
Hawthorne in his views on reform and reformist zeal.

The Salem *Register* reviewed Hawthorne's *The Scarlet Letter* on March 21, 1850, and expressed its obvious displeasure
with the Custom House sketch. In this prefatory sketch,
Hawthorne attacked the Salem Whig leaders, particularly
Charles W. Upham, for having him removed from his post
at the Salem Custom House after the election of Zachary

Taylor, a Whig. The Whig *Register* wrote that it could not
understand how any "gentleman" could have made such
a "venemous, malignant, and unaccountable assault" on
Upham. Hawthorne's justification for attacking that "vil-
lain," Upham, went beyond the political scene. Upham had
visited Concord shortly after the Hawthornes were married
and he returned to Salem with stories that the young couple
was living in abject poverty. Although it was true that the
Hawthornes had little or no money and were living on vege-
tables from their garden, the situation did not warrant such
gossip.[5] More importantly, Hawthorne may have had, as some
critics have suggested, a much more profound artistic purpose in writing the Custom House sketch, and he might have
revealed a deep-seated personal resentment against Salem's
social structure, morality, and historical significance in writing the Custom House sketch.

This same review in the *Register* also strangely refers to
Hawthorne's "transcendentalism": "Indeed, while reading
the chapter on the Custom House, we almost begin to think
that Hawthorne had mistaken his vocation—that, instead of
indulging in dreamy transcendentalism, and weaving exquisite
fancies to please the imagination and improve the heart, he
would have been more at home as a despicable lampooner,
and in that capacity would have achieved a notoriety which
none of his tribe, either of ancient or modern times, has
reached." Here "transcendentalism" may refer to the movement per se; however, it seems likely that what was meant
was fancy, fantasy, or imagination, as the word was used as a
synonym for these terms. The reviewer had linked Hawthorne
to the Transcendentalists on aesthetic principles; later critics
would, of course, do the same.

On March 25, 1850, the *Register* quoted a passage on the
same subject from an out-of-town newspaper: "We could
readily believe that our author was entirely out of place here—
he who had fellowshipped 'with the dreamy brethren of
Brook Farm'—who had lived 'for three years within the sub-

tile influence of an intellect like Emerson's'—who had indulged in 'fantastic speculations' with Ellery Channing—talked with Thoreau in his hermitage—grown 'fastidious by sympathy with the classic refinement of Hillard's culture'—and became imbued with poetic sentiment at Longfellow's hearth-stone." The source of this statement is not known but it seems clear that the writer felt that Hawthorne had absorbed much too much of the Transcendental spirit to have ever written the Custom House sketch. More importantly, the statement may also be implying that this kind of writing is what comes of living with such men. Salem was apparently in agreement with this assessment of Hawthorne and, undoubtedly, the editor who published it sought to show that Salem's citizens were not alone in their feelings and were not overreacting. The quotation from the Custom House sketch used in the article is something of a distortion, however, for it stops short of where Hawthorne states his desire for a different kind of company: "It was time, at length, that I should exercise other faculties of my nature, and nourish myself with food for which I had hitherto had little appetite. Even the old Inspector was desirable, as a change of diet, to a man who had known Alcott. I look upon it as an evidence, in some measure, of a system naturally well balanced, and lacking no essential part of a thorough organization, that, with such associates to remember, I could mingle at once with men of altogether different qualities, and never murmur at the change."[6] Of course, the review wished to narrow Hawthorne's philosophic and social views, to categorize and label him.

Julian Hawthorne wrote that the publication of *The Blithedale Romance* drew favorable response from many of Hawthorne's friends.[7] He cites a letter from William Pike of Salem who "probably knew Hawthorne more intimately than any other man did": "In this book, as in 'The Scarlet Letter,' you probe deeply,—you go down among the moody silences of the heart, and open those depths whence come motives that give complexion to actions, and make in men what are called states of mind; being conditions of mind which cannot be removed either by our own reasoning or by the reasonings of others."[8] Pike's enthusiasm, modified by his own Swedenborgianism and his close friendship with Hawthorne, is not, again, representative. In general, critical responses to the novel were more plentiful in England. Considering that at the time of Hawthorne's death only one thousand copies of the novel had been printed, the lack of any great response is understandable.[9]

In September 1838, there occurred a series of events in Salem that had dramatic dimensions and considerable importance for a study of the reaction of Salem to the Transcendental movement.[10] Jones Very was at the center of the action, which also involved two prominent Salem ministers, Charles W. Upham and John Brazer, as well as Elizabeth Palmer Peabody and Ralph Waldo Emerson. The significance of these events is derived largely from biographical information concerning the two ministers as well as letters revealing their attitudes toward Transcendentalism in general, the *Divinity School Address,* and the miracles question, in particular, letters which each minister had written almost two years earlier to Andrews Norton, the foremost Unitarian of the day.

Charles Wentworth Upham (1802–1875) was pastor of the First Church of Salem for twelve years. He had graduated from Harvard in 1821 and from the Cambridge Divinity School in 1824.[11] He was a friend of Emerson's at Harvard where they were both in the same literary club (1819).[12] After the lyceum movement had started, Upham invited Emerson on April 3, 1836, to lecture at the Salem Lyceum. On November 5, 1836, Upham wrote to Norton to express support for Norton's almost single-handed stand against Ripley during the miracles controversy. Upham said that although his friend Ripley had to be censured he felt much easier now that someone had spoken out against Transcendentalism, which he considered " 'absolutely and not remotely, of infidel tendency and import.' "[13]

The other Salem minister, John Brazer (1789–1846), had graduated first in his class from Harvard in 1813.[14] He became a professor of Latin at the college and then, in 1820, became pastor of the North Church. In 1836, Harvard granted Brazer a D.D. degree, and he then served on the Board of Overseers. Brazer contributed numerous articles and reviews to the *North American Review* and the *Christian Examiner,* and in 1835 he was invited to deliver the Dudleian Lecture at Harvard.[15] In a biographical sketch of Brazer in the *Dictionary of American Biography,* Merle E. Curti offers some interesting comments on Brazer's philosophic and religious attitudes: "Brazer's point of view was symptomatic of the forces which crystallized in Transcendentalism. His Dudleian Lecture (May 13, 1835) anticipated Emerson's *Nature* and *Divinity School Address* in denying that the great truths of religion can be ascertained through *a priori* reasonings or metaphysical assumptions. . . . Brazer's lucid exposition of doctrines that have been considered Emersonian before Emerson's own formulation of them, gives him a definite though minor place in the history of American thought."[16] Although he cites short phrases from Brazer's works, Curti uses little material from the Dudleian Lecture itself. The interpretation of this lecture depends largely on tone—an ironic and undercutting tone that seems to have eluded Curti. Considering all that we know of the man, we can safely assume that Brazer would have been shocked by a sketch of his life that put him in league with Emerson.[17]

On November 7, 1836, two days after Upham had written his letter to Norton, Brazer wrote to Norton and said that he had written to the *Christian Examiner,* the leading Unitarian journal, to ascertain the editorial policy of that publication. Brazer felt that the journal had become far too liberal and permissive toward the new views, which he clearly thought were not in the best interests of the Unitarian Church. Brazer seems to have been jumping on the anti-Transcendental bandwagon since, as he said, he had not read Ripley's article (which had leaned toward Transcendentalism) but could tell "what its import [was]." The articles that Brazer objected to in the *Examiner*, as best he could remember, were the ones on the Resurrection and on Swedenborg. Brazer also told Norton that he had not liked Brownson's praise of Carlyle, of whom he also admitted that he had no knowledge. Brazer knew, however, that those who supported the views of Carlyle were those who endangered the morals of the community.[18] It was just this kind of uncritical thinking and shallow conservatism that made the relationship between the two ministers and Jones Very all the more unfortunate.

On Sunday morning, September 16, 1838, Jones Very, the Transcendentalist sonneteer who had returned to Salem from his post as Greek tutor at Harvard, began to make a number of visits to people in Salem. He was still in the throes of a nervous collapse. He went to Elizabeth Peabody's house where he announced the coming of Christ, a service he had also performed for all of Harvard College and which had been the cause of his removal from Harvard. Very repeated passages from the twenty-fourth chapter of the Gospel of Matthew and then drifted into his own interpretation of the text in the rhetoric of the King James Version of the Bible. Elizabeth Peabody, who was so much in awe of what was happening, did not perceive the shift. When he had finished, Very casually slipped into a matter-of-fact conversation similar to other conversations he had had with Elizabeth. Elizabeth later learned that Very had stopped first at the homes of Lucius Bolles, Charles W. Upham, and his own minister, John Brazer, whose church Very had recently joined. Very's intention was to announce the coming of Christ. According to Elizabeth Peabody, during Very's encounter with Brazer and Upham, Brazer was

ninny enough to ask this poor crazy youth for the *miracles* that tested his mission. Very said "this revelation would not have miracles." "Then," said Mr. B. "I must say to you—you are laboring under hallucination! &c." . . .

Two [ministers] had resisted him. [Lucius] Bolles—the Baptist minister—had actually put him bodily out of the house, and Mr. [Charles Wentworth] Upham, who at that time was a good deal excited against the transcendentalists, calling Mr. Emerson an Atheist—and declaring that it was wrong to listen to him,—had told Mr. Very that he should see that he be sent to the Insane Asylum.[19]

Elizabeth went to Upham to dissuade him from his intentions, but ever since Emerson had published *Nature*, Upham had been strongly opposed to the Transcendentalists. Upham blamed Emerson for Very's state of mind, and, as he knew Elizabeth Peabody to be a friend of Emerson's, he was unimpressed by her pleas. Very was sent to the insane asylum the following day.

Elizabeth wrote the following revealing letter to Emerson on October 20, 1838:

I suppose you have heard of Jones Very's insanity—and very like in an insulting way—for Satan seems to be let loose upon you—and all the people are gone rabid—(I mean the people who have hold of the *press*) . . . Mr. Brazer— (the doubly distilled old woman)[20] —goes on and talks to him about working miracles to prove his mission—or yielding the same that he is insane.—Since [Very] has come home [Brazer] has been telling him that *you* (from whom Mr. B. affects to believe all the thing comes) are *now* universally acknowledged to be denounced as an *atheist*—and measures are taking!! to prevent you from having any more audience to corrupt. . . . Miss Burley and I spent an hour or two together the other day chiefly talking of you—and our sympathies moral intellectual and religious [are] with you—which the more we understand you the more we feel;—and rejoicing to hear that you had said "none of the dirt thrown upon you sticks to you"—for even *you* cannot make your friends so *sublime* as not to *feel* some degree of tenderness for the *mass* of flesh and blood and part of "that *tissue*" so mysteriously called the human heart.[21]

Elizabeth was angry because Very had brought criticism

down upon Emerson, but she was, in turn, happy that Emerson was not taking that criticism very seriously. She was, nonetheless, surprised by the reactions of Salem's leading citizens and the severity of the action taken against Very. Why had Brazer and particularly Upham, who had gone only so far as to write anti-Transcendental letters of support to Norton, become so upset at Very's disturbance? Why had these men, one of whom was a college classmate of Emerson's and had never attacked him in print, placed so much responsibility on him now? Clearly, Very, as a member of Brazer's church, was visible proof of the ill effects of the Transcendental philosophy and was a very real threat to the Unitarian establishment and a rebel of the worst kind. Emerson had stayed clear of the miracles controversy once he had begun it with his *Divinity School Address*. It might well be imagined that Upham and Brazer felt that they had Emerson on good evidence this time and could draw him openly into the controversy. A reason had to be offered to the people of Salem for Very's extreme behavior, and Emerson was given the role of Transcendental scapegoat. Very himself was convinced that there was a conspiracy against him and Emerson.[22] No written evidence, other than that provided by Elizabeth Peabody, is available to support the idea that Salemites in general felt Emerson to be culpable. His name is conspicuously absent from the Salem Lyceum syllabi until February 1840, however.

The difficulty arising from incidents in Salem in 1838 points to a more subtle but ultimately very important set of relationships. The relationship between literary figures of Salem and authors outside of Salem, mainly in Concord, is important because it points in a more general way to the values that Transcendentalism as a movement tried to introduce into Salem and what effects these efforts had upon the literature produced both there and elsewhere.

It might be helpful to consider first a friendship and artistic relationship that existed within Salem. The reaction to Jones Very and his chimerical behavior by Salem's leading

citizens and the sympathy of Elizabeth Peabody for Transcendentalism is known, but what of the other literary giant
in Salem, Nathaniel Hawthorne? What were his reactions
to Very, Elizabeth Peabody, Emerson, and Thoreau? How
much was Hawthorne influenced by the lyceum, its lecturers,
and Transcendentalism? How deeply did all of these relationships affect Hawthorne's writing?

Hawthorne's connection to the Transcendental spirit was
no less than the relationship he had with his wife. Although
Sophia Hawthorne was not an avowed Transcendentalist,
her temperament as well as her philosophic inclinations
made clear her sympathies. Her spiritual and aesthetic sen-
sibilities were not so much the result of a choice of Transcendental beliefs (as opposed to those of her husband) as they
were a product of her sister Elizabeth's influence on her.
If Transcendentalism was amorphous and difficult to grasp,
Hawthorne's aesthetics and philosophy approached mys-
teriousness. Sophia Hawthorne could perhaps see similarities
that were less obvious to others and could reconcile the two
conflicting philosophies and artistic viewpoints. More importantly, she could see the similarity between the emphasis
placed on the intangible by both her husband and the Transcendentalists. Whether the attitudes were gloomy or benign
was perhaps not as important to her as the fact that the intangible, unseen forces affecting mankind were the proper
domain of the artist.

Nathaniel Hawthorne was ever mindful and respectful of
Elizabeth Peabody's learning and intellectual powers. She
made herself known to the Hawthorne family after she had
read several sketches and had learned that one of the Hawthornes had written them. When she went to congratulate
the author of the sketches, she was greeted at the door by
Louisa Hawthorne. Elizabeth Peabody told Louisa Hawthorne
that her sister Elizabeth Hawthorne must be a genius for
writing such stories. Louisa replied that the caller must be
mistaken, for it was her brother Nathaniel who had written

the stories. Miss Peabody replied that if that was the case he should not remain "idle." Little did she know, of course, how busy Hawthorne actually was at this time.

From that time onward Elizabeth Peabody numbered Nathaniel Hawthorne among her discoveries. She invited him to the Peabody house, introduced him to Mary and Sophia, and made sure that he was invited to Miss Burley's house. In short, she drew him out of his seclusion. During Hawthorne's term as surveyor at the Boston Custom House, Elizabeth operated her Boston bookstore and encouraged him to publish under her imprint a collection of children's stories and biographies, *Grandfather's Chair, a History for Youth*, which she had recommended he write while they were both still living in Salem.[23] Emerson's concern for biography and its didactic benefits and Elizabeth Peabody's consequent encouragement of Hawthorne in the same area are more than coincidence and indicate what an important link between Transcendentalism and Hawthorne she was. It is difficult to tell just how much more influence Elizabeth Peabody had on Hawthorne during his residence in Boston, but even if it was no more extensive than has been recorded she brought Hawthorne much closer to society. Hawthorne, however, was quiet and reserved and he seems never to have understood Elizabeth's social nature and gregariousness. Paradoxically she cared little for social amenities. She was not neat, and consequently she offended on occasion.[24] This attitude was not only uncharacteristic for a New Englander, it was unfeminine. Furthermore, Elizabeth Peabody encouraged Sophia Hawthorne in the belief that Emerson was the greatest man alive, a belief that irritated Hawthorne more than a little.

Sophia Peabody had met Emerson when he had made a trip to Salem in April 1836. She was impressed by his lecture and his manner. After their friendship had begun, Emerson asked her to cast a medallion of his brother Charles who had just died. She entered upon the task with enthusiasm and accomplished the work very much to Emerson's satisfaction. Sophia Peabody also made a visit to Concord to see Emerson, and when *Nature* first appeared she read it and praised it in a letter to Emerson.

Sophia Peabody's idealism was not experiential but was based on her reading of Fénelon, Gerando, Plato, and Xenophon.[25] Often Elizabeth Peabody's acquaintances and friends became hers, and Sophia's connection to the Transcendental movement can be seen in her friendship with Dr. William E. Channing, James Freeman Clarke, Frederic Hedge, George Ripley, and Margaret Fuller. She corresponded with Amos Bronson Alcott concerning Carlyle, Schiller, and Sampson Reed's *Growth of the Mind.*[26]

Since Elizabeth Peabody had taken a special interest in Jones Very as she had Nathaniel Hawthorne earlier, it was not only inevitable that these two men should meet but that the meeting should be arranged by her and take place in her home. Both men arrived at the Peabody residence on the evening of January 3, 1838, to escort Elizabeth Peabody to the Salem Lyceum. Sarah Freeman Clarke, a guest of Elizabeth Peabody's at the Peabody home, recalled that Hawthorne " 'shrouded in a cloak, Byronic and very handsome, looked gloomy, or perhaps only shy.' "[27]

Hawthorne and Very took a liking to each other but it was a cautious and guarded relationship, especially on Hawthorne's side. His natural insularity thwarted Very's attempts at a more intimate relationship even though the two men were to meet frequently in the parlors of Salem's leading bluestockings, Miss Susan Burley and Mrs. Caleb Foote. Very often called at Hawthorne's home; since he did so without an invitation, he did not endear himself to Hawthorne. It is difficult to know what Very sought in the friendship; it might be supposed that he would have been happy to pierce some layers of Hawthorne's aloofness and look at the man's mind. Furthermore, Very wanted Hawthorne to be "a kind of spiritual brother," much to the latter's embarrassment.[28]

In November 1838, Very was ready to deliver his "mission" (this time that he himself was the second Christ) to Hawthorne, an act of love he had bestowed on Elizabeth Peabody in September of that same year and which resulted in his temporary confinement. Writing to Emerson, Elizabeth Peabody told him how Hawthorne received the ceremony:

> Hawthorne received it in the loveliest manner—with the same abandonment with which it was given—for he has that confidence in truth—which delivers him from all mean fears—and it was curious to see the respect of Very for *him*—and the reverence with which he treated his genius. There is a petulance about Hawthorne generally—when truth is taken out of the forms of nature . . . though the happiest and healthiest physical nature tempers it—so that it only expresses itself on that one occasion. But in this instance he repressed it and talked with him beautifully.[29]

Hawthorne's attitude toward Very changed somewhat after this strange encounter, and he became more sympathetic. Very was, however, always too obvious, too loud, in his avowal of friendship, to Hawthorne's annoyance. The basis of the increased understanding between these two men seems to have been their unique position in relation to Salem's society. As Edwin Gittleman has said, this new understanding is

> clarified through an independent description by Elizabeth of the story-collection Hawthorne projected in 1833 and recalled five years later in connection with Very: "In it [the narrator] describes himself as a gloomy idler who could not make up his mind to get into any profession, and a neighbor of his, as much at a loss as himself for a worldly vocation, who was a religious enthusiast, with an idea that he was sent by God on a mission to call the world to a higher life. These two exceptional Yankees were tabooed by the prosaic community from which they were dissidents; and this brought them into a strange intimacy."[30]

That this "prosaic community" was indeed Salem and that

Hawthorne and Very, the implied subjects, were "dissidents" needs no further support than Very's encounter with Upham and Brazer and the suspicion, real or imagined, that was directed against Hawthorne as a mysterious artist-type during the investigations of the White Murder Case in 1830.[31] The artist's position in society seems to have been just as difficult then as it is now; in fact, the general attitude in those times was more justified because of people's inexperience with the artist's life-style. What is important is that Hawthorne and Very felt the pressure of the scrutiny intensely, and this fact perhaps caused them to identify more easily with one another. As regards their friendship on the personal level, Hawthorne's knowledge of the high esteem that Sophia Peabody had for Jones Very did little to simplify his attitude toward the Salem sonneteer. There is, however, a strong indication that Hawthorne felt Very to be an excellent poet, a fact which in his mind would have surely taken precedence over Very's eccentricities and Hawthorne's own personal reservations.[32]

The historical reconstruction of the Very-Upham controversy and the Very-Hawthorne friendship reveals a perplexing matrix from which it is difficult to draw conclusions concerning personal attitudes, especially Hawthorne's. The matrix was of real interest to Hawthorne as a writer, however, for there is evidence to suggest that he made the events of 1838 the basis for his short story "Egotism; or, The Bosom Serpent." Robert Arner offers some very convincing evidence for seeing the character of Elliston, the protagonist in this story, as being based upon Very, but Arner is most interesting in the summation of the evidence he presents:

> That Hawthorne intended to satirize Very's isolation is obvious; equally obvious, however, is that many of Elliston's victims in the story are guilty of hypocrisy, that they deserve the rough treatment they receive at his hands. So Hawthorne's irony is sometimes directed at Elliston, sometimes at the townspeople. Perhaps the most revealing portion of the story for an evaluation of Hawthorne's probable

position is the ending. Though Elliston possesses all the vices of Hawthorne's great villains, Hawthorne arranges for him alone a reunion with reality and the world of men; the past, dismal as it was, is allowed to throw no gloom upon the future. It may be that this difference can best be explained by recognizing that Very, not Elliston, is on Hawthorne's mind at this point. The moral commitment he might have felt was not to a created character in a created milieu, but to a real person whom he knew, a person whose sincerity he respected at the same time that he rejected the conclusions to which that sincerity seemed to lead.[33]

When Hawthorne came to know Emerson, Hawthorne was no longer living in Salem, yet his ties to that town were so strong that his reaction to Emerson and his beliefs may be to a certain degree representative of Salem and, therefore, it is useful to trace Hawthorne's relationship to Emerson even after the former's Salem years. Hawthorne's feelings toward Emerson showed much the same reserve that characterized his relationship with Very. In 1839 Sophia Peabody was living in Salem and Hawthorne was working at the Boston Custom House. She wrote and encouraged him to hear Emerson lecture. He replied: "Dearest, I have never had the luck to profit much, or indeed any, by attending lectures; so that I think the ticket had better be bestowed on somebody who can listen to Mr. Emerson more worthily."[34] In "The Old Manse," the opening sketch of *Mosses from an Old Manse*, Hawthorne says that he "admired Emerson as a poet of deep beauty and austere tenderness, but sought nothing from him as a philosopher,"[35] and Mark Van Doren explicated this statement: "Hawthorne was too accurate a judge of persons to miss in Emerson the quality of his charm. Nobody with imagination ever missed that. But for Hawthorne it could be no more than personal. The intellect of Emerson had less than nothing to give him, just as nothing that came out of his own imagination—out of its depths, at least—could be of meaning to Emerson."[36] These distortions eventually found their way into the early studies of Hawthorne. Recent scholarship, however, has sought to bring Hawthorne's political and social interests into proper perspective and to see more similarities and even some influence between Hawthorne and Emerson.[37]

Although Sophia Peabody had had close initial contact with Emerson, it was not until the newly married Hawthornes moved into the Manse in Concord that a real friendship began between Emerson and the Hawthornes. The intellectual mantle that was worn so long by Channing had now fallen upon Emerson's shoulders, and Emerson had become famous. Hawthorne was respectful of that fame, which gave yet another dimension to his naturally reserved character. Of course, Emerson was delighted by the arrival of the couple because Hawthorne was another important literary figure who would enhance the Concord group that already included such figures as Alcott, Thoreau, William Ellery Channing II, Charles Lane, and Emerson himself. All along Emerson had felt that Concord could be a much more natural, realistic, and practical intellectual community than Brook Farm: a community that could give inspiration and stimulation but that could also insure working time, privacy, and freedom.

Hawthorne wrote that Emerson was one of the first persons to enter into the sacred inner circle of joy that characterized his marriage. Hawthorne and Emerson walked and talked together and made a journey to the nearby Shaker community in Harvard, a trip that separated Hawthorne from his wife for the first time since their marriage. On a later occasion, when Sophia Hawthorne was away for a visit, Emerson and Hawthorne had some serious conversations that deepened their friendship.[38] There might be some truth in the notion that Sophia Hawthorne's enthusiasm for Emerson made it difficult for her husband to appraise the man for himself and that moments of greater understanding were brought about by her absence.

There is little evidence to indicate at what point exactly Emerson became interested in Hawthorne's works, but in

September 1842, Emerson wrote in his diary that Hawthorne's works were not good for anything and it was, in fact, a tribute to Hawthorne that they were not.[39]

During the summer of Hawthorne's second year in Concord, Emerson read the anti-Transcendental short story "The Celestial Railroad" and enjoyed it very much. In a letter to Thoreau dated January 10, 1843, Emerson comments on his reading of the story: "Hawthorne walked with me yesterday p.m. and not until after our return did I read his 'Celestial Railroad' which has a serene strength which one can not afford to praise,—in this low life."[40] Emerson apparently showed no signs of annoyance at the description of one of the characters in the story, Giant Transcendentalist.[41]

Hawthorne never criticized Emerson personally. To the contrary, he paid him a great tribute by acknowledging his importance in the character of Ernest in "The Great Stone Face." Hawthorne says of Ernest: "If he sang of a mountain, the eyes of all mankind beheld a mightier grandeur reposing on its breast, or soaring to its summit, than had before been seen there. . . . The Creator had bestowed him, as the last best touch to his own handiwork. Creation was not finished till the poet came to interpret, and so complete it."[42] Indeed, Hawthorne found much that was attractive in Transcendental thought: its self-reliance, its psychology, its antimaterialism, its rejection of institutionalized religion, its concern for symbols, and, finally, its attempts to get closer to the true nature of reality and existence. Two stories, "The Threefold Destiny" and "The Great Stone Face," illustrate another Transcendental concern of Hawthorne's, the divinely inspired common man.

While they lived in Concord, the Hawthornes began a friendship with one other important Transcendentalist, Thoreau, who, like Emerson, was one of the first visitors the Hawthornes had at the Old Manse. "When he came to dine late in August, Hawthorne saw him as a singular character— as ugly as sin, long-nosed, queer-mouthed, and with rustic yet courteous manners which corresponded very well with his exterior."[43] Although Hawthorne referred to *The Dial* as a soporific,[44] he liked Thoreau's "Natural History of Massachusetts," which had appeared in *The Dial*, because of Thoreau's ability to combine a concern for metaphysics, poetry, and close scientific observation, a synthesis that was also characteristic of the great seventeenth-century English prose writers. Thoreau sold Hawthorne his rowboat and taught him how to row. The finesse and charm that Thoreau could bring to this simple exercise was for Hawthorne an emblem of Thoreau's inner being. Perhaps, most enjoyable for Hawthorne were the talks he had with Thoreau at Walden in which Thoreau spoke so absorbingly about nature and Indian lore, subjects in which he had great expertise. Hawthorne, however, not so surprisingly, never really opened his heart or home to Thoreau. The period of closest contact with Thoreau was the summer before the Hawthornes left Concord, and that fact may have had some bearing on the intimacy of the relationship.

In addition, Terence Martin says that in the 1850s Thoreau told Hawthorne the story of a man who believed himself to be deathless and Hawthorne had hoped to write a sketch of Thoreau for the preface to *The Dolliver Romance* in which he had incorporated the idea. "The preface would discharge 'the duty of a live literary man to perpetuate the memory of a dead one.' "[45] Hawthorne never completed the romance, however, and the manuscript of the work lay on his coffin at his funeral. Hawthorne's intention seems to go beyond a literary debt and to show some greater respect for Thoreau, a respect that even historical evidence may never accurately reveal to us.

There were other meetings, influences, and exchanges of ideas between Hawthorne and the Transcendentalists in Concord. There was, for example, the famous meeting of Emerson, Hawthorne, and Margaret Fuller in Sleepy Hollow to which Margaret Fuller brought a volume with a strange title (perhaps Kant's *Critique of Pure Reason*).[46] This meeting took place on the spot that would one day be Hawthorne's final resting place—a meeting and setting that would be paralleled in *The Blithedale Romance*. Hawthorne's interest in society and in his contemporaries after his sojourn at Brook Farm was clearly burgeoning and, although that interest corresponded to the awakening that was taking place in Salem, it was, given his artistic temperament, a highly personal response.

In summary, Salem's reaction to Transcendentalism is evidenced in the short, barbed criticisms that found their way into the Salem newspapers, the reviews of Emerson's lectures also found there, the later assessment of Emerson by Henry K. Oliver, those immediate responses by Upham and Brazer to Very's announcement of the second coming, the sympathies of Elizabeth and Sophia Peabody, and the relationship between literary figures inside as well as outside Salem—Hawthorne's relationship with the Peabodys and Very and Emerson and Thoreau chiefly. It is clear that this reaction was neither overtly hostile nor very enthusiastic for the commercially oriented Salem.

NATHANIEL HAWTHORNE

SOMEWHERE between the statement by John Erskine that "the romances of Hawthorne can hardly be understood apart from the current of Transcendentalism in which his genius was formed"[1] and the statement by Henry Seidel Canby that "Transcendentalism as such touched him not at all"[2] lies the true character of the influence and effect of Transcendentalism on Hawthorne. Hawthorne himself assessed the influence of Transcendentalism and his position relative to it in an introductory paragraph that he added in 1854 to "Rappaccini's Daughter." He refers to himself as M. de l'Aubépine (French for Hawthorne):

> As a writer, he seems to occupy an unfortunate position between the Transcendentalists (who, under one name or another, have their share in all the current literature of the world) and the great body of pen-and-ink men who address the intellect and sympathies of the multitude. If not too refined, at all events too remote, too shadowy, and unsubstantial in his modes of development to suit the taste of the latter class, and yet too popular to satisfy the spiritual or metaphysical requisitions of the former, he must necessarily find himself without an audience, except here and there an individual or possibly an isolated clique.[3]

As a writer, Hawthorne positioned himself somewhere between the popular tastes and the Transcendentalism of his age, but this statement does not actually reveal his moral and aesthetic beliefs nor does it tell very much about his attitudes toward reform and Transcendentalism. Transcendentalism served Hawthorne in several important ways. It gave him support for his individualism and helped him formulate his ideas on the relative power of good and evil. Hawthorne gave a dark ending to *The Scarlet Letter* because he felt that was the only way such a dark story could end. More importantly, he wished to show the power of blackness because that was a part of his very being and because the Transcendentalists overemphasized, in his judgment, the power of good and de-emphasized evil. The fact that the pre-Transcendental stories lack the powerful themes of "Young Goodman Brown," "Rappaccini's Daughter," "The Birthmark," and especially *The Scarlet Letter* supports this view.

In addition to giving some indication of his religious beliefs, Hawthorne's early sketches dealing with the supernatural and with American history and legend contrast nicely with the sketches in *Mosses from an Old Manse* and show an important developmental trend in Hawthorne's work—a development influenced by Transcendentalism. His new concern was satire, and more specifically criticism of Transcendentalism. His new technique was allegory, an attempt to deal less directly with the objects of his satire. The important sketches in this new concern by Hawthorne with contemporary attitudes were "The Celestial Railroad," "The Procession of Life," "The Birthmark," "The Hall of Fantasy," "The Christmas Banquet," "Rappaccini's Daughter," "A Select Party," and "Earth's Holocaust." These stories, which were written mostly between the years 1843 and 1846, were published in 1846 as *Mosses from an Old Manse* when the Hawthornes were living in Concord.

"The Celestial Railroad," which has as its model John Bunyan's *Pilgrim's Progress*, is an allegorical satire in which Hawthorne replaces Pope and Pagan with the monster Giant Transcendentalist. With both tongue-in-cheek and a marked air of seriousness he describes that figure:

He is a German by birth, and is called Giant Transcendentalist; but as to his form, his features, his substance, and
his nature generally, it is the chief peculiarity of this huge
miscreant that neither he for himself, nor anybody for him,
has ever been able to describe them. As we rushed by the
cavern's mouth we caught a hasty glimpse of him, looking
somewhat like an ill-proportioned figure, but considerably
more like a heap of fog and duskiness. He shouted after us,
but in so strange a phraseology that we knew not what he
meant, nor whether to be encouraged or affrighted.[4]

But it is difficult to tell just how serious Hawthorne was in his
creation of Giant Transcendentalist. His not very specific
description of the figure echoes the oftvoiced criticism of both
the amorphousness of the Transcendental movement and the
vapidity of its rhetoric. "The Celestial Railroad" also makes
the point that things are different in the modern age when
people can use the convenience of the train to help them
carry their sins. They do not have to suffer in quite the same
way that Christian, forced as he was to carry his sins on his
back, had to suffer in *Pilgrim's Progress*. Of course, what Hawthorne is saying is that there is no easy way to a pure heart or
easy conscience no matter what modern conveniences, that
is, current philosophy or religion, would lead you to believe.

In "The Procession of Life," Hawthorne attempts to arrange
groups of people according to categories, love and intelligence, for example, that are more reasonable than those
produced within a social structure. In so doing, he gives
us a way of looking at all of the tales and sketches in *Mosses*
and that is to see them as "processionals" for the way in which
they mechanically and rather obviously draw across the stage
of life the social issues and problems that Hawthorne felt
compelled to examine. He also gives another example of his
attitude toward reform, particularly that characteristic of the
reformer that he will show us through Hollingsworth in *Blithedale*: "When a good man has long devoted himself to a particular kind of beneficence—to one species of reform—he is apt

to become narrowed into the limits of the path wherein he treads, and to fancy that there is no other good to be done on earth but that selfsame good to which he has put his hand, and in the very mode that best suits his own conceptions."[5] In 1836, Hawthorne recorded in his notebook an idea for a story involving a reformer that indicates that his attitudes were the same even at this early date: "A sketch to be given of a modern reformer,—a type of the extreme doctrines on the subject of slaves, cold water, and other such topics. He goes about the streets haranguing most eloquently, and is on the point of making many converts, when his labors are suddenly interrupted by the appearance of the keeper of a mad-house, whence he has escaped. Much may be made of this idea."[6]

In "The Birthmark," Alymer, a man of science, rejects humanity as he finds it in favor of what he hopes to make of it. Alymer becomes obsessed with the birthmark, a diminutive hand, on the cheek of his beloved wife Georgiana, which is an emblem for him of her "liability to sin, sorrow, decay, and death."[7] Alymer wishes the mark removed and his obsession with it so absorbs Georgiana that, out of her great love for him, she allows him to attempt the removal of the mark. By administering a series of medications, Alymer succeeds in removing the birthmark from his wife but only at the cost of her life. He has allowed his shortsighted monomania to get the better of him: "The momentary circumstance was too strong for him; he failed to look beyond the shadowy scope of time, and, living once for all in eternity, to find the perfect future in the present."[8] Hawthorne implies that the pursuit of perfection necessitates the removal or destruction of all that is imperfect. Failure to recognize imperfection is a failure to recognize existence itself. Hawthorne does not overtly condemn the man of ideas. Alymer had a profound and noble vision but he erred greatly in ignoring the forces of reality represented by his earthly assistant: "Then a hoarse, chuckling laugh was heard again! Thus ever does the gross fatality of earth exult in its invariable triumph over the immortal essence which, in this dim sphere of half development, demands the completeness of a higher state."[9] The relationship between the moral of the sketch and the Transcendentalists' refusal to admit the power of evil or death into their conception of existence seems obvious.

The major concern of the next sketch, "The Hall of Fantasy," is the world of the imagination and Hawthorne's mixed feelings toward it. The hall, which holds the same relationship to the world of imagination as does the Bourse or Exchange for the commercial world, is an effective metaphor. The narrator tells us that even though the hall may have to be modified to suit future ages, it "is likely to endure longer than the most substantial structure that ever cumbered the earth,"[10] and those who " 'have affairs in that mystic region, which lies above, below, or beyond the actual, may here meet and talk over the business of their dreams.' "[11] In the hall rest the busts of some of the establishment's past officers: Homer, Dante, Shakespeare, Milton, Bunyan, Scott, and America's Charles Brockden Brown. Hawthorne's narrator almost wishes that he could spend the rest of his life in the hall that is so beautifully colored by the light that filters through its stained glass windows. There are dangers, however, for some mistake the hall for " 'actual brick and mortar,' "[12] and others live there exclusively and thus make themselves unfit for the "real employments of life."[13] After numerous arguments for and against life in the hall, the narrator realizes the need to visit the place only occasionally. Hawthorne makes the point that imagination and fancy are most effective as they are set against the backdrop of reality—that to live in the imaginative and idealistic world exclusively, as the Transcendentalists did, was to lead a less than total life.

"The Hall of Fantasy" makes the most explicit comments that Hawthorne ever offered on his Transcendental contemporaries. In an excellent article, "Hawthorne Surveys His Contemporaries," Harold P. Miller makes reference to an earlier version of "The Hall of Fantasy," which appeared in

James Russell Lowell's *The Pioneer* in February 1843, some three years prior to its inclusion in *Mosses.*[14] In the earlier version of the sketch, the members of the hall are mentioned by name, and Hawthorne's remarks are more explicit. Among those cited are Alcott, Brownson, Emerson, and Very, and the sketch makes reference to numerous unnamed Brook-Farmers as well as to many of the most prominent thinkers of the day. "Of the Brook-Farmers, with whom he had only recently severed relations, he speaks courteously; they are the 'old friends . . . with whom, though a recreant now, I had borne the heat of many a summer's day, while we labored together towards the perfect life. They seemed so far advanced, however, in the realization of their idea, that their sun-burnt faces and toil-hardened frames may soon be denied admittance to the Hall of Fantasy.' "[15] A friend of Hawthorne's narrator in this early version talks of Bronson Alcott:

" 'Here is a prophet,' " cried my friend, with enthusiasm— " 'a dreamer, a bodiless idea amid our actual existence. Another age may recognize him as a man; or perhaps his misty apparition will vanish into the sunshine. It matters little; for his influence will have impregnated the atmosphere, and be imbibed by generations that know not the original apostle of the ideas. . . . Such a spirit cannot pass through human life, yet leave mankind entirely as he found them!' "[16]

Jones Very is described as being " 'within a circle which no other of mortal race could enter, nor himself escape from.' "[17] In this suppressed version, Hawthorne speaks of Emerson as

surrounded by an admiring crowd of writers and readers of the Dial, and all manner of Transcendentalists as disciples of the Newness, most of whom betrayed the power of his intellect by its modifying influence upon their own. He had come into the hall, in search, I suppose, either of a fact or a real man; both of which he was as likely to find there as elsewhere. No more earnest seeker after truth than he, and few more successful finders of it; although, sometimes, the truth assumes a mystic unreality and shadowyness in his grasp.[18]

The most important question raised is why Hawthorne decided to change this earlier version of "The Hall of Fantasy." Miller offers several possible answers.[19] Hawthorne through his narrator says in the first version: " 'But, woe is me! I tread upon slippery ground, among these poets and men of imagination, whom perhaps it is equally hazardous to notice, or to leave undistinguished in the throng.' "[20] Hawthorne was, in short, still reserved and somewhat politic. He wanted a better reception for *Mosses* than had been accorded *Twice-Told Tales.* Furthermore, according to Miller, Hawthorne did not seem to have the proper motivation in this critique—the kind of justification or stature that would later prompt Hawthorne's treatment of certain individuals in the Custom House sketch. Miller rules out any aesthetic consideration in the revision: "It is unlikely that any delicate artistic motive influenced the revision, since Hawthorne did not take trouble to mend the gaps which were left by the omissions. As the narrative appears in *Mosses,* praise and disparagement of reformers and writers stand awkwardly side-by-side, because intervening paragraphs have been dropped."[21] Considering Hawthorne's attitudes in other sketches from *Mosses* under discussion here, this "awkwardness" that Miller senses seems very much in keeping with Hawthorne's middle-of-the-road indecisiveness.

A more recent article makes further use of the earlier version of "The Hall of Fantasy" and Miller's research to suggest a number of interesting points about Hawthorne's stay at the Old Manse during the writing of *Mosses* and, more importantly, his relationship with Thoreau at that time. In " 'The Hall of Fantasy' and the Early Hawthorne-Thoreau Relationship," Buford Jones goes beyond R. W. B. Lewis's passing reference and Frank Davidson's earlier work on the influence of

Thoreau on *Mosses* and indicates that Hawthorne and Thoreau had a greater rapport and spiritual kinship than has hitherto been realized.[22] Jones also points to the interest each man had in the literary endeavors of the other with the strong suggestion that Hawthorne identified with Thoreau in a way that he never could have with Emerson. Hawthorne had praised Thoreau in "The Old Manse" and "The Custom House" as well as in his journal: "He is a good writer—at least, he has written one good article, a rambling disquisition on Natural History in the last Dial—which, he says, was chiefly made up from journals of his own observations. Methinks this article gives a very fair image of his mind and character—so true, minute, and literal in observation, yet giving the spirit as well as letter of what he sees, even as a lake reflects its wooded banks, showing every leaf, yet giving the wild beauty of the whole scene."[23] Hawthorne certainly liked Thoreau's analytical mind, but he also saw mirrored in Thoreau something of himself—that same strong, independent nature that has come to characterize Hawthorne.

The major thrust of Jones's thesis is that Thoreau influenced Hawthorne in the writing of not only "The Hall of Fantasy" but also *The House of the Seven Gables* and *The Blithedale Romance*. Hawthorne similarly influenced Thoreau's thinking about Alcott and Emerson, perhaps even causing Thoreau to see Alcott as a more important thinker than Emerson. Thoreau's writing of "The Landlord" and "Paradise (to be) Regained," a review-article, both of which appeared in the *Democratic Review*,[24] was also influenced by Hawthorne.

In "The Christmas Banquet" Hawthorne presents himself, or himself as he used to be, as Gervayse Hastings.[25] The story is important for its attacks on reformers and also for its denunciation of insensitivity, especially as it reflects Hawthorne's own attitude toward Transcendentalism. Roderick, the narrator, explains in his short introduction to the sketch how he sees Gervayse: " 'He looks like a man; and, perchance, like a better specimen of man than you ordinarily meet. You might esteem him wise; he is capable of cultivation and refinement, and has at least an external conscience, but the demands that spirit makes upon spirit are precisely those to which he cannot respond. When at last you come close to him you find him chill and unsubstantial—a mere vapor.' "[26] The main portion of the sketch concerns the will of a "certain old gentleman" who requests that "ten of the most miserable persons that could be found" be invited every year to a Christmas banquet. The guest list changes every year but Gervayse, who is perplexingly free of any semblance of misery, but who is, much to Hawthorne's point, free of any feeling whatever, is the only perennial guest.

Several guests who attend the banquet during Gervayse's eightieth year are of special interest. One was a former clergyman described in the following manner:

> But, yielding to the speculative tendency of the age, he had gone astray from the firm foundation of an ancient faith, and wandered into a cloud region, where everything was misty and deceptive, ever mocking him with a semblance of reality, but still dissolving when he flung himself upon it for support and rest. His instinct and early training demanded something steadfast; but, looking forward, he beheld vapors piled on vapors, and behind him an impassable gulf between the man of yesterday and today, on the borders of which he paced to and fro, sometimes wringing his hands in agony, and often making his own woe a theme of scornful merriment. This surely was a miserable man.[27]

Another guest was "a theorist who had conceived a plan, by which all the wretchedness of earth, moral and physical, might be done away, and the bliss of the millennium at once accomplished. But, the incredulity of mankind debarring him from action, he was smitten with as much grief as if the whole mass of woe which he was denied the opportunity to remedy were crowded into his own bosom."[28] Another guest at the banquet, Father Miller, who had predicted the end of the world in one final conflagration, also finds his way into several other sketches in *Mosses*.

A philanthropist, also in attendance, asks Gervayse, who by this time has gained a reputation for his presence at these banquets, just what generalizations about misery he can make from his long experience. Gervayse replies that he knows nothing except his own misery—the misery of having no feelings at all. What Hawthorne implies here is that as difficult as the speculative philosopher, the theorist, or even Father Miller are to understand, they are not nearly as puzzling as Gervayse's dilemma. Roderick says of Gervayse at the end of the sketch: " 'Of such persons—and we do meet with these moral monsters now and then—it is difficult to conceive how they came to exist here, or what there is in them capable of existence hereafter.' " [29]

As Hubert Hoeltje has pointed out, three characters were "awaiting the gestation of Time" before they appeared as actors in a drama that would more fully discuss the questions raised by these stories in *Mosses*. They are "a modern philanthropist, too sensible of the calamities of thousands and millions of his fellow creatures to have the heart to do the little good that lay immediately within his power; a half-starved, consumptive seamstress; and a woman of unemployed energy, who found herself in the world with nothing to achieve, and brooding over the wrongs of her sex—the prototypes of Hollingsworth, Priscilla, and Zenobia of *The Blithedale Romance*, as yet hardly conceived . . . ." [30]

In addition to his remarks made by way of comparison to his contemporaries (ministers who left the Unitarian Church, reformers, and millenarians) in "The Christmas Banquet," Hawthorne seems to refer to his own period of isolation prior to his association with Brook Farm. Again, he expresses the moderate view that to live in the material world exclusively is at best only equal to a life led solely in the world of fantasy. More likely, it is something less than that.

"Rappaccini's Daughter" echoes "The Birthmark" in the endeavor of Giacomo Rappaccini to scientifically protect his daughter from sin and from evil by enveloping her in that very evil. The story is a complex one and, therefore, stands out among the rather simple allegories that make up most of *Mosses*. It contains an inner and outer story that are brought to a simultaneous conclusion. In the main story, Rappaccini, a doctor, has made his daughter Beatrice poisonous and keeps her in an inaccessible garden. Giovanni Guasconti, a young medical student living at the Rappaccini house, falls in love with Beatrice and is eventually made poisonous himself by the girl's father in order that she might have a companion. The inner story involves a conflict between Rappaccini and Pietro Baglioni, a doctor at the nearby university. They are in professional competition and use basically different investigative techniques. Baglioni attempts to convince Giovanni that Rappaccini is using the young man as an experiment and that he cares little for human life. Baglioni is equally contemptible, however. He cares little for human life himself and also uses Giovanni as an experiment. It is typical of Hawthorne's writing that those who have the clearest vision are precisely those who seek to violate their fellow men.

When Beatrice finally asks her father why he has inflicted this "miserable doom" on her, he replies: " 'What mean you, foolish girl? Dost thou deem it misery to be endowed with marvellous gifts against which no power nor strength could avail an enemy—misery, to be able to quell the mightiest with a breath—misery, to be as terrible as thou art beautiful? Wouldst thou, then, have preferred the condition of a weak woman, exposed to all evil and capable of none?' " Beatrice answers that she " 'would fain have been loved, not feared.' "[31] Rappaccini is guilty of a lack of faith in the power of love and a pure heart. He is very much concerned about his daughter's welfare but mistakenly believes that the only way to survive in a sinful world is to be more sinful than one's fellow man. Beatrice is, of course, Hawthorne's spokesman in her expression of the belief that love might have been a better answer. Rappaccini is another character in Hawthorne's fiction who

seeks to violate others. There seems to be a connection between such violators and the reformer's zeal that looks at
others' faults rather than at one's own. Again, Hawthorne's
caveat is that the answer lies in one's heart.

The entire sketch "A Select Party" is concerned with the
dangers of entering the world of the imagination, the world
of Transcendentalism, even as a guest. The story tells of "a
Man of Fancy" who "made an entertainment at one of his
castles in the air, and invited a select number of distinguished
personages to favor him with their presence."[32] The guest
list included "the Oldest Inhabitant," a magician, and "a
number of guests whom incredulous readers may be inclined
to rank equally among creatures of imagination."[33] Among
this group was a "Reformer untrammelled by his theory."[34]
There is also a Master Genius, a figure whom the country
awaits "to fulfil the great mission of creating an American
literature"[35] and to whom is eventually given the seat of
honor. The entire group tours the castle of the air but does
not take nearly so much delight in its airy entertainments as
it does in the "more solid as well as liquid delights of the festive
board."[36] Hawthorne satirizes visionaries in general but is
most severe at the end of the sketch when these people desire
to return to earth: "How, in the darkness that ensued, the
guests contrived to get back to earth, or whether the greater
part of them contrived to get back at all, or are still wander-
ing among the clouds, mists, and puffs of tempestuous wind,
bruised by the beams and rafters of the overthrown castle in
the air, and deluded by all sorts of unrealities, are points that
concern themselves much more than the writer or the public.
People should think of these matters before they thrust themselves on a pleasure party into the realm of Nowhere."[37]

The sketch "Earth's Holocaust" projects a period when a
huge bonfire is lit by the inhabitants of the world in order to
eliminate the "trumpery" that has overburdened the planet.
As the story progresses, more and more is thrown into the
fire until a man of "stately presence" rushes in and cries:

" 'People, what have you done? The fire is consuming all that marked your advance from barbarism, or that could have prevented your relapse thither.' "[38] One of the comments directed by the narrator at his contemporaries satirizes the feminist movement and Elizabeth Peabody and Margaret Fuller by implication: "It somewhat startled me to overhear a number of ladies, highly respectable in appearance, proposing to fling their gowns and petticoats into the flames, and assume the garb, together with the manners, duties, offices, and responsibilities, of the opposite sex."[39] The narrator also recalls the burning of a volume of poems: "I especially remember that a great deal of excellent inflammability was exhibited in a thin volume of poems by Ellery Channing."[40] All the world's books are thrown on the fire, and as a comfort to a poor "bookworm" whose life is now without object the narrator mockingly echoes Emerson's statement in *Nature*: " 'Is not Nature better than a book?' "[41] The crowd gathered at the fire finally succeeds in pushing a gallows into the flames in a desperate attempt to do away with death. Here again the Transcendental failure to recognize reality is Hawthorne's target: " 'Death, however, is an idea that cannot easily be dispensed with in any condition between the primal innocence and that other purity and perfection which perchance we are destined to attain after travelling round the full circle; but, at all events, it is well that the experiment should now be tried.' "[42]

As the narrator begins to realize that everything in the world is being destroyed and that life appears to be gloomier than ever, he is given reassurance that not everything of value will be consumed in the flames. His companion tells him that people have forgotten to throw one thing into the flames and this oversight has rendered all their activity meaningless. That one item is the human heart: " 'And, unless they hit upon some method of purifying that foul cavern, forth from it will reissue all the shapes of wrong and misery . . . .' "[43] The narrator contemplates the truth that his friend has uttered and the patent misdirection of the reformers:

> Purify that inward sphere, and the many shapes of evil that haunt the outward, and which now seem almost our only realities, will turn to shadowy phantoms and vanish of their own accord; but if we go no deeper than the intellect, and strive, with merely that feeble instrument, to discern and rectify what is wrong, our whole accomplishment will be a dream, so unsubstantial that it matters little whether the bonfire, which I have so faithfully described, were what we choose to call a real event and a flame that would scorch the finger, or only a phosphoric radiance and a parable of my own brain.[44]

Hawthorne kept a diary and notebooks when he lived at the Old Manse in which he revealed how *Mosses,* like his earlier sketches, would be a sourcebook for his future works. He recorded there the name Pearl, a pretty name for a girl he thought. Hawthorne was later to join this casual notebook entry with the young woman who wore a scarlet *A* on her bosom in "Endicott and the Red Cross" to produce Hester and her daughter of *The Scarlet Letter.*

In 1850, Hawthorne published *The Scarlet Letter,* a novel rich in its treatment of the dichotomy of good and evil and the psychological effects of wrongdoing on the human psyche. The resolution of the story and the technique Hawthorne uses to accomplish that resolution are important because the novel can be read as an anti-Transcendental work in its emphasis on the power of evil. *The Scarlet Letter* was greatly influenced by Hawthorne's earlier short story writings. He had most recently written "Ethan Brand" and the idea of the "unpardonable sin," of a sin against the heart, was still of great interest to him.

Very near the beginning of the novel Hawthorne writes: "The founders of a new colony, whatever Utopia of human virtue and happiness they might originally project, have invariably recognized it among their earliest practical necessities to allot a portion of the virgin soil as a cemetery, and another portion as the site of a prison."[45] The importance of this statement goes beyond its function in the novel and makes an observation on Brook Farm and communities like it, where the denial of the darker side of life was, as far as Hawthorne knew, historically unprecedented. After the death of Zenobia, Coverdale says, "Blithedale, thus far in its progress, had never felt the necessity of a burial-ground."[46] The Boston of *The Scarlet Letter* began as a utopia but it had an important attachment to reality; it considered the eventuality of death and of misdeeds. What Hawthorne says through Coverdale is that the Blithedalers had no need for a cemetery because no one died; more importantly, he implies that there was no cemetery because no one thought about the possibility of death. The Blithedalers' attempt to modify Zenobia's burial rites proved to be impossible. Tradition had to be followed, and this fact lends further support to Hawthorne's belief that there are certain basic truths that cannot be changed or denied and that man's solace in this instance lies in his acceptance of, and reliance on, these truths.

Hawthorne's imagery and characterization are the most important techniques he employs in *The Scarlet Letter*. The imagery itself operates on two planes, the natural and the moral. Throughout the novel Hawthorne balances natural good and natural evil, using flowers, particularly the rose, and weeds to illustrate the equality of nature. On the moral or human level, moral evil stands alone in this Puritan society where moral good is repressed if not denied altogether.[47]

Although the four main characters in the novel, Hester, Dimmesdale, Chillingworth, and Pearl, are complex, their movements throughout the course of the novel are clearly defined. Hester, much scorned in the beginning of the novel, gradually rises and appears finally to transcend her suffering. Dimmesdale, initially obscure and seemingly innocent, sinks to a great depth of despair and then almost miraculously rises to confront his sin before the Puritan society. Chillingworth follows a path that leads to pure evil and depravity. He is akin to the Paul Pry figure of *The Blithedale Romance* and guilty of the "unpardonable sin," a sin much worse than that committed by Hester and Dimmesdale.[48] Pearl, a strange mixture of innocence and wildness, is her mother's child and must reach maturity outside the bounds of the novel.

The character of Hester is as interesting as it is complex. She shows tremendous strength throughout the novel, and as Hyatt Howe Waggoner has said, Hawthorne "created in Hester a somewhat Transcendental heroine."[49] Some readers have interpreted the A that she wears to stand for Angel rather than Adultress, and Hawthorne himself, who sees her as nunlike, a "Sister of Mercy,"[50] says that some people in the novel saw the A as signifying Able.[51] Hester shows herself to be bigger than her problems and rises almost by dint of her sin. She shows a tendency to slight the darker side of life, to ignore the "ruined wall," the "unpardonable sin," and in so doing she seems to win Hawthorne's admiration. Waggoner goes so far as to say that "she had been literally forced into practicing Emerson's greatest virtue, self-reliance, in the insolation of her 'magic circle of ignominy.' "[52] In the chapter "The Child at the Brook-side," Hester talks of the fact that the forest cannot hide her letter and sin but that " 'the mid-ocean shall take it from [her] hand, and swallow it up forever' " as she and Dimmesdale plan to run away together. It is here that Hawthorne shows his readers how little sense of reality she possessed in thinking that her heart could be made pure again.

The ending of the novel makes it clear that the mixture of good and evil, of the light and dark natures of Hester, Dimmesdale, and Pearl, are no match for the power of the pure black heart of Chillingworth. There is no real indication that Hester and Dimmesdale can escape their sin or that Pearl's character will ever change. Hawthorne emphasized two points here. One is that there is no escape from sin despite what religion would have us believe, and the other is that the search for good in evil, as Chillingworth learns, is destructive.

Hawthorne, in *The Scarlet Letter,* came down heavily on the dark side of human nature for many reasons not the least of them being the de-emphasis by the Transcendentalists of that aspect of existence.

The House of the Seven Gables was published in 1851, the year after the publication of *The Scarlet Letter.* The theme of the second novel, or romance as Hawthorne preferred to call it in his famous Preface, is the influence of the past upon the present, symbolized by Maule's curse upon the Pyncheons, a fictionalized rendering of the curse on Hawthorne's ancestor John Hathorne. Set against this force of the past is the self-reliance of the young "reformer" Holgrave, himself a Maule, and Phoebe, and Hepzibah and Clifford Pyncheon, Phoebe's aunt and uncle. That self-reliance in Holgrave is offset by Hawthorne's proverbial view of the reformer. He says of Holgrave's attack on outmoded institutions: "His error lay in supposing that this age, more than any past or future one, is destined to see the tattered garments of Antiquity exchanged for a new suit, instead of gradually renewing themselves by patchwork; in applying his own little life-span as a measure of an interminable achievement; and, more than all, in fancying that it mattered anything to the great end in view whether he himself should contend for it or against it."[53]

In the chapter "The Flight of Two Owls," Hepzibah and Clifford flee from the House of the Seven Gables where Judge Pynchon, who had intended to have Clifford declared insane in order to take over his property, has just visited them and died, symbolizing the end of Maule's curse. Hepzibah and especially Clifford are euphoric as they boldly strike out late in their lives to experience life itself. They are representative of Transcendental flight and freedom, especially as Clifford stands in opposition to an acquaintance he makes on board the train carrying them away from the town. This man represents a conservative view of human development and may be seen as symbolic of the reaction to Transcendentalism. For instance, the only use the man can imagine for the newly developed telegraph is to aid in the capture of bank robbers and murderers, whereas Clifford would use it differently: " 'Lovers, day by day,—hour by hour, if so often moved to it,—might send their heart-throbs from Maine to Florida, with some such words as these, 'I love you forever!'—'My heart runs over with love!'—'I love you more than I can!' and, again, at the next message, 'I have lived an hour longer, and love you twice as much!' " [54] Of course, his acquaintance thinks that Clifford is insane.

Clifford makes these comments on the train itself and on human progress in general:

> "It has just occurred to me, on the contrary, that this admirable invention of the railroad—with the vast and inevitable improvements to be looked for, both as to speed and convenience—is destined to do away with those stale ideas of home and fireside, and substitute something better. . . ."
>
> "You are aware, my dear sir,—you must have observed it in your own experience,—that all human progress is in a circle; or, to use a more accurate and beautiful figure, in an ascending spiral curve. While we fancy ourselves going straight forward, and attaining, at every step, an entirely new position of affairs, we do actually return to something long ago tried and abandoned, but which we now find etherealized, refined, and perfected to its ideal. The past is but a coarse and sensual prophecy of the present and the future." [55]

F. O. Matthiessen says of this portion of "The Flight of Two Owls" that "Hawthorne ironically makes [Clifford] develop the transcendental doctrine that evil is bound to disappear in the ascending spiral of human improvement." [56] Clifford says that the present and the future have always been a return to the past and that the past has always been difficult to escape entirely. It would seem to Clifford, however, that the linearity of the train and the great mobility it provides may either be a great change or at least symbolize such a change. Clifford continues this discussion, which is more of an essay by Hawthorne than a conversation between two fellow passengers: " 'In the early epochs of our race, men dwelt in temporary huts, of bowers of branches, as easily constructed as a bird's-nest, and which they built,—if it should be called building, when such sweet homes of a summer solstice rather grew than were made with hands.' "[57] That was the charmed life, says Clifford, and we can have it again because " 'they gave us wings; . . . they spiritualize travel!' "[58] Why, asks Clifford, should any man build an abode that he cannot carry on his back as did the earlier races? The two owls, of course, are Hepzibah and Clifford, and with the train they carry their nest with them. The home symbolizes for them Maule's curse, tradition, inculcation of the past, and a form of death. Hawthorne will use again the figures of the bower and the bird's nest in *The Blithedale Romance,* where they will symbolize security and provide for another opportunity for the voyeurism of Coverdale. Hawthorne has already put Clifford in the position of a Paul Pry in an earlier scene where Clifford peers down from his window on a passing band and has to be restrained from throwing himself into the crowd below, from destroying himself by immersing himself in life itself.[59] The way Hawthorne, through Clifford, feels about the noise and rumbling of the train is much the same way that Thoreau felt about trains, and the ideas expressed here concerning shelter and the virtue of carrying one's house around with him are exactly those of Thoreau in *Walden* and may be a further product of the earlier friendship of Hawthorne and Thoreau. Thoreau never felt, however, that the train could provide for anything like the flight of the soul.[60]

The resolution of the conflict of the novel is indicated by the image of the owl. In the beginning of the chapter that follows "The Flight of Two Owls," Hawthorne refers to the owl as that creature that is "bewildered in the daylight, and hasten[s] back to his hollow tree" where it is comfortably dark.[61] When Hepzibah and Clifford finally get off the train they are at a desolate way-station where only an abandoned church and house can be seen in the darkness. They are frightened, and Hepzibah kneels down and prays to God to have mercy on them. They have valiantly struck out into life, but there is the strong suggestion that like an owl they have spent so much time in darkness they may not be able to adjust to the light. Hawthorne seems to say that every effort must be made to throw off the past, that it must be done early in life, perhaps as Holgrave and Phoebe have done, and that the road ahead is not easy. Hawthorne discusses just how difficult the trip is in his next work, *The Blithedale Romance,* which reflects and comments on his experiences at Brook Farm ten years earlier.

On April 12, 1841, Nathaniel Hawthorne became a member of Brook Farm, the Transcendental utopian community in West Roxbury, Massachusetts, eight miles from Boston. His decision to join the community caused no great stir at the time when enthusiasm about such ventures was running high. Viewed retrospectively, however, Hawthorne's membership in that community was very much out of character for him, and it has become one of the most perplexing problems for both the biographer and the critic of his writings.

Brook Farm was one of the many projects undertaken by the members of the Transcendental Club, or Symposium as it was sometimes called, and no utopian or socialistic project that existed in the first half of the nineteenth century has been so well remembered or chronicled as the Brook Farm community. On November 9, 1840, George Ripley wrote to Ralph Waldo Emerson to give him a more detailed idea of the project that he as its progenitor had in mind:

> Our objects, as you know, are to insure a more natural union between intellectual and manual labor than now exists; to combine the thinker and the worker, as far as possible, in the Same individual; to guarantee the highest mental freedom, by providing all with labor, adopted to their tastes and talents, and securing to them the fruits of their industry; to do away the necessity of menial services,

by opening the benefits of education and the profits of labor to all; and thus to prepare a society of liberal, intelligent, and cultivated persons, whose relations with each other would permit a more simple and wholesome life, than can be led amidst the pressure of our competitive institutions. [62]

It is difficult to imagine the quiet, remote, and at times shy Hawthorne fitting into the communal and social activities that were so much the essence of life at Brook Farm. It is more difficult to imagine Hawthorne going to Brook Farm to do physical labor as was one of Ripley's hopes for intellectuals at the community. The fact of the matter is that Hawthorne from the start enjoyed both the socializing and the farmwork that he did, but his motivation for joining the community was only partially related to either of these activities. His basic desire was to find there a way of providing himself with an income and time to write. He had been engaged to Sophia for two years and had been unable to find a way of supporting himself so that they could marry. On April 13, 1841, the day after he arrived at Brook Farm, Hawthorne wrote to Sophia: "Think that I am gone before, to prepare a home for my Dove, and will return for her, all in good time." [63] Brook Farm offered at least a glimmer of hope in the solution of his problems.

Not long afterward Sophia visited Hawthorne at Brook Farm and knew immediately that the life there was not for him. Hawthorne's letters from Brook Farm reveal his growing disillusionment, and Arlin Turner traces it for us: "After ten days at the farm: 'It is an endless surprise to me how much work there is to be done in the world.' After three weeks he wrote of shoveling manure in what he called the goldmine: 'It defiles the hands, indeed, but not the soul.' After six weeks: 'It is my opinion that a man's soul may be buried and perish under a dung-heap, or in a furrow of the field, just as well as under a pile of money.'" [64] In August, some five months after he became a member of the community, Hawthorne changed his status and became a boarder there with the hopes that he

might be able to succeed by making less of a physical commitment. Failing this, he decided that it was impossible for him
to be connected with the community in any way. He left before the arrival of winter.

More than ten years after his stay at Brook Farm Hawthorne set forth his beliefs concerning social reform in *The
Blithedale Romance,* beliefs that he never offered in his non-
fiction writings or utterances. Hawthorne states in his Preface
to *Blithedale* that he does not "put forward the slightest pretentions to illustrate a theory, or elicit a conclusion, favorable
or otherwise, in respect to socialism."[65] He also says that inas-
much as readers will recognize the setting as Brook Farm, he
would not wish them to make any close identification of
fictional characters in the romance with actual members of
the Brook Farm community.

It is obvious to the student of the period that in *Blithedale*
Hawthorne created something of a *roman à clef.* Identifica-
tions of real people can be made, but with no great degree
of certainty and with even less purpose. There are many
possible models for each character in the work, and even if it
could be proven that a certain person was the model for Hollingsworth, for instance, it is unlikely that such information
could lead us to a greater understanding of *The Blithedale
Romance.*[66]

One notable identification, however, has been somewhat
more productive in dealing with the novel—the relationship
between the narrator Miles Coverdale and Hawthorne himself.
Coverdale is Hawthorne's only sustained first-person narrator;
and, although the differences between them far exceeded their
similarities, there are parallels between Coverdale's situation
and Hawthorne's at Brook Farm that are interesting. Coverdale and Hawthorne are both literary men who seek among
other things the opportunity to write, to experiment with their
lives, and to engage in a progressive social experiment with
the realization that a certain amount of physical labor will
be required of them. They both arrive at their respective com-

munities, get feverish colds, and are nursed back to health. Both are moved by the pastoral landscapes and are proud that they can do physical labor, but both feel degraded and finally depressed by that labor. How much each of them seeks to reform society, an ostensible purpose of both communities, is an interesting question. Coverdale does not understand how it is to be accomplished; Hawthorne never really says that reform is one of his motives. It is also strange that both Coverdale and Hawthorne have come out of solitude to become a part of a larger solitude. Both men finally become disillusioned; we might best understand the cause and effect of that disillusionment as well as other parallels between Coverdale and Hawthorne by an analysis of both Coverdale and *The Blithedale Romance*.

Miles Coverdale, a bachelor with no visible means of income, is fond of fine food, sherry, and cigars. He says he quests for a better way of life.[67] He has all the material amenities that anyone could hope for, but he obviously seeks something more. The irony of his situation is that he really does know just what it is that he seeks. It is brotherhood; but, strangely enough, he will not commit himself to others. He is a Transcendentalist, a poet, and a reader of Emerson, Carlyle, and *The Dial*.[68] He does very little writing at Blithedale or in town; nor does he, strangely enough, show any concern or unhappiness about his lack of artistic productivity. The question of his commitment to his art raises the larger and more important question of his commitment to Blithedale, or to his fellow man. When he is asked by Moodie in the beginning of the romance if he would do him a favor, Coverdale hesitates indicating that he would rather not and then asks, "'A very great one?'" When Moodie lets Coverdale know that he is aware of his standoffishness, Coverdale suddenly becomes very interested. Coverdale's change is motivated, so he says, by the prospect of becoming involved with a woman[69] (indeed Coverdale's sexual attitudes are an interesting topic in themselves), but this change is characteristic of the ironic attraction-repulsion syndrome he exhibits throughout the work. The delicate balance that Coverdale maintains between involvement and aloofness is curious. He is attracted by the experiment of Blithedale but does not really wish to take part fully in it. Very near the end of the work he says: "Yet, were there any cause, in this whole chaos of human struggle, worth a sane man's dying for, and which my death would benefit, then—provided, however, the effort did not involve an unreasonable amount of trouble—methinks I might be bold to offer up my life. . . . Further than that, I should be loath to pledge myself."[70]

Interestingly, Coverdale throughout the romance makes extensive use of dramaturgical metaphors as he equates life at Blithedale to an imitation of reality or life.[71] References to curtains, veils, masks, actors, acting, role playing, and masquerades indicate that Coverdale sees Blithedale as a pastoral entertainment, an Arcadia. All drama is an imitation, yet it is essential to see that it creates its own reality as well; it is equally important to see Coverdale's involvement and withdrawal as being intimately connected with the levels of reality that are inherent in the dramatic element of *Blithedale*. Coverdale begins his narrative as an observer and then gradually becomes an actor in the drama. In so doing he maintains his role as audience as well as actor, or as he himself puts it:

My own part in these transactions was singularly subordinate. It resembled that of the Chorus in a classic play, which seems to be set aloof from the possibility of personal concernment, and bestows the whole measure of its hope or fear, its exultation or sorrow, on the fortunes of others, between whom and itself this sympathy is the only bond. Destiny, it may be,—the most skilful of stage-managers,— seldom chooses to arrange its scenes, and carry forward its drama, without securing the presence of at least one calm observer. It is his office to give applause when due, and sometimes an inevitable tear, to detect the final fitness of incident to character, and distil in his long-brooding thought the whole morality of the performance.[72]

Finally, Coverdale achieves another level of distance as he plays the more objective role of narrator. He either regulates his distance from the action himself or has it regulated for him as in the scene in town when he stands in his apartment and peers down into the apartment occupied by Zenobia.[73] She sees him, drops the curtain on the window, and cuts him off from the action entirely. Coverdale becomes so disturbed that he finds himself knocking on Zenobia's door before he realizes it. He has become so quietly angry that he is subsumed by that anger; his action is spontaneous and mechanical. He is invited in by Zenobia and is then ignored by both Zenobia and her guests, Priscilla and Hollingsworth. He nevertheless puts such a damper on the action that it virtually ceases until Zenobia, Priscilla, and Hollingsworth leave.

As has been frequently pointed out, Coverdale is the clearest manifestation of the Paul Pry figure, a figure who lives off the actions of others through his voyeurism. In "Sights from a Steeple" (1831), Hawthorne wrote: "The most desirable mode of existence might be that of a spiritualized Paul Pry, hovering invisible round man and woman, witnessing their deeds, searching into their hearts, borrowing brightness from their felicity and shade from their sorrow, and retaining no emotion peculiar to himself."[74] Three other major manifestations of this figure occur in Hawthorne's fiction: the artist in "The Prophetic Pictures," Clifford in *The House of the Seven Gables*, and Kenyon in *The Marble Faun*.

Early in the first chapter of *The Blithedale Romance*, Coverdale says he asked the Veiled Lady for her assessment of the prospects for the success of Blithedale. "The response, by the by, was of the true Sibylline stamp—nonsensical in its first aspect, yet, on closer study, unfolding a variety of interpretations, one of which has certainly accorded with the event."[75] The response is enigmatic. It means everything and, therefore, nothing, and as the romance ends, Coverdale is no closer to an understanding of Blithedale than the Veiled Lady was capable of giving. If Blithedale is Brook Farm, then it was a failure.

But there is no evidence in the romance other than its obvious failure for the main characters, that the community actually collapses. Nevertheless, the overriding impression one gets from what Coverdale says of the prophecy is that the future of Blithedale is not bright or hopeful.

Coverdale's real unhappiness and cynicism throughout the work are in great evidence and carry much importance if we see him as an autobiographical figure for Hawthorne. In a passage from the novel that reflects the differing attitudes of Coverdale at the time he left for Blithedale and when he writes his narrative, Coverdale indicates his awareness that the passing of time has tarnished the hope he once had:

> The better life! Possibly, it would hardly look so, now; it is enough if it looked so then. The greatest obstacle to being heroic is the doubt whether one may not be going to prove one's self a fool; the truest heroism is to resist the doubt; and the profoundest wisdom to know when it ought to be resisted, and when to be obeyed.
>
> Yet, after all, let us acknowledge it wiser, if not more sagacious, to follow out one's day-dream to its natural consummation, although, if the vision have been worth the having, it is certain never to be consummated otherwise than by a failure. And what of that? Its airiest fragments, impalpable as they may be, will possess a value that lurks not in the most ponderous realities of any practicable scheme. They are not the rubbish of the mind. Whatever else I may repent of, therefore, let it be reckoned neither among my sins nor follies that I once had faith and force enough to form generous hopes of the world's destiny,—yes!—and to do what in me lay for their accomplishment: even to the extent of quitting a warm fireside, flinging away a freshly lighted cigar, and travelling far beyond the strike of city clocks, through a drifting snow-storm.[76]

Yet, shortly after this, in recounting the journey to Blithedale, Coverdale says that a friend told him not to "'laugh at what little enthusiasm [he had] left,'" indicating that even then he was considered skeptical by those around him.[77] At another point, Coverdale again reflects on the differing attitudes he has concerning reform: "In my own behalf, I rejoice that I could once think better of the world's improvability than it deserved. It is a mistake into which men seldom fall twice in a lifetime; or, if so, the rarer and higher is the nature that can thus magnanimously persist in error."[78] He is also bothered by the material necessity of having to compete soon after his arrival at Blithedale in the Brighton fair pig sale and by his belief that the Blithedalers would not enjoy the experiment if given a choice about joining.[79] His point is that such an experiment says nothing about those who are forced into such a way of life without choice. Coverdale worries about the singularity and narrowness of Hollingsworth's plans for the reformation of criminals. He says of Hollingsworth: "He ought to have commenced his investigation of the subject by perpetrating some huge sin in his proper person, and examining the condition of his higher instincts afterwards."[80] Coverdale's thoughts about the success of making a more complete man, of mixing labor and intellectualism at Blithedale, are revealed in the following passage and are reminiscent of what Hawthorne had to say about Brook Farm:

> The clods of earth, which we so constantly belabored and turned over and over, were never etherealized into thought. Our thoughts, on the contrary, were fast becoming cloddish. Our labor symbolized nothing, and left us mentally sluggish in the dusk of the evening. Intellectual activity is incompatible with any large amount of bodily exercise. The yeoman and the scholar—the yeoman and the man of finest moral culture, though not the man of sturdiest sense and integrity—are two distinct individuals, and can never be melted or welded into one substance.[81]

Coverdale never feels that he can give himself over completely or freely to his consociates, and the only place he can write poetry or think about an essay for *The Dial* is in his hermitage. This hideaway in the branches of a white pine tree is the equivalent of a human-sized bird's nest and is womb-like. It offers him a retreat within a retreat, a Blithedale of his very own, and it is not coincidental that Hawthorne, who had gone to Brook Farm to provide a basis for marriage, thought of it as a perfect honeymoon spot. Here is Coverdale's description of his hideaway:

> Long since, in this part of our circumjacent wood, I had found out for myself a little hermitage. It was a kind of leafy cave, high upward into the air, among the midmost branches of a white-pine tree. A wild grapevine, of unusual size and luxuriance, had twined and twisted itself up into the tree, and, after wreathing the entanglement of its tendrils almost around every bough, had caught hold of three or four neighboring trees, and married the whole clump with a perfectly inextricable knot of polygamy. Once, while sheltering myself from a summer shower, the fancy had taken me to clamber up into this seemingly impervious mass of foliage. The branches yielded me a passage, and closed again beneath, as if only a squirrel or bird had passed. Far aloft, around the stem of the central pine, behold a perfect nest for Robinson Crusoe or King Charles! A hollow chamber of rare seclusion had been formed by the decay of some of the pine brances, which the vine had lovingly strangled with its embrace, burying them from the light of day in an aerial sepulchre of its own leaves. It cost me but little ingenuity to enlarge the interior, and open loopholes through the verdant walls. Had it ever been my fortune to spend a honeymoon, I should have thought seriously of inviting my bride up thither, where our next neighbors would have been two orioles in another part of the clump.[82]

It is clear throughout *The Blithedale Romance* that Coverdale is sexually frustrated and that this frustration is a part of his overall lack of commitment and his desire for solitude balanced against his desire for society. The juxtaposition of these forces is culminated in Coverdale's final annoying confession: "I—I myself—was in love—with—PRISCILLA!"[83]

Coverdale is a parody of Hawthorne himself, yet in that parody there is a great deal of truth. Coverdale is lost in the conclusion of the romance. His cynicism has permitted him to stand by and watch the destruction of that part of the community that was most meaningful to him. When his world is lost, Coverdale, an essentially parasitic character, is lost as well; and he is the one to blame for that loss. Coverdale's occasional probes into the private lives of his friends may have speeded their tragedies, and he is then both the agent and the victim of his own noninvolvement. Coverdale's total assessment of the project, derived from the less than optimistic tone of the narrative written some years after the experience, is not an easy matter to determine. He is pleased to think that he was once more optimistic than he now is, but equally pleased to note that his perception of the difficulties and inconsistencies of Blithedale was accurate. Yet, in the end, Coverdale has lost Priscilla and has failed to make any connection with society at all. Coverdale is not Hawthorne, nor is Hawthorne Coverdale. Coverdale is an exaggeration; he has problems peculiar to himself and his story. As Hawthorne's persona, however, Coverdale does reflect some of the problems Hawthorne himself had in assessing his experience at Brook Farm. Writing for both men appears to be an attempt to unravel the skein of ironies that is their experience, yet that attempt is largely unsatisfactory. To label the experience good or bad, optimistic or pessimistic, or succcessful or unsuccessful would be to distort the reality of it. It was a story that was very well suited to the form and mode of a romance because it remained for Hawthorne a veiled and mixed experience.

It was not until 1860 that Hawthorne published *The Marble Faun*, his last novel. Written after Hawthorne had lived abroad for some time, *The Marble Faun* thus reflects less of the Transcendental spirit. Yet, R. W. B. Lewis sees in Donatello, as he does in Clifford of *The House of the Seven Gables*, another manifestation of the new Adam. Donatello's personality before his fall is given in images of Eden by Hawthorne and by Kenyon, Hilda, and finally by Miriam herself after Donatello's crime. Donatello's fall is a re-enactment of Adam's fall and is put finally in terms of a *felix culpa*, not because like the first fall it brought about the coming of Christ but for some purely secular advancement, the attainment of conscience. Donatello has been a mysterious character, the personification of innocence, of unworldly innocence prior to his fall. His recognition of the importance of the past, of the fact that man has already sinned once, and of how the past can influence one's life is discussed by Lewis:

> The action has to do with the discovery of *time* as a metaphor of the experience of evil. Rome is thus the best imaginable setting; nothing in the New World could match it. What was wanted, for the maximum effect, was maximum antiquity— a symbol coexistent, if possible, with the temporal order itself; and Rome is identified in the story as "the city of all time." The seven-gabled home of the Pyncheons had reached back a century or so to the Puritan period, and Hawthorne did all he could with it. But Rome, Hawthorne remarks on the opening page of *The Marble Faun*, reaches back through a "threefold antiquity"—Christian, Roman, Etruscan. And it is in dramatic contrast to such massive age that the hero is then promptly introduced as an "Arcadian simpleton." . . . In *The Marble Faun*, the action unfolds from its starting point: in terms of Donatello's consciousness of the quality, the content, the pressures of time. It is thus only *after* the sin and the flight that Donatello seems to grow aware of his own ancestry—explaining to Kenyon, at Monte Beni, that his family history goes back beyond the Middle Ages to earliest Christendom and perhaps to a time before that.[84]

The Marble Faun, then, is as temporally removed from *Blithedale* as Hawthorne was able to make it. Hawthorne seems to be saying in this work that Donatello is better for his sin, that he is finally a man and not removed from life itself. The ending of the work is not totally unsatisfactory as viewed from that

standpoint. The white innocence of Hilda would seem to inter-
fere with that ending, however. Presumably Hawthorne's
sympathies should lie with this fictionalized personification
of those qualities that he admired in his wife, Sophia, yet
Hilda comes across as a rather unreal, sterile character incapable of feeling. She is similar to the innocent Donatello,
and Hawthorne seems incapable of identifying with either
experience or such innocence. Hawthorne has moved his
characters to a setting and placed them in a temporal relation
that should have made his resolution more natural, but the
ending of *The Marble Faun* is as veiled as the ending of *The
Blithedale Romance*.

Hawthorne changed his emphasis in his movement from
Twice-Told Tales to *Mosses from an Old Manse, The Scarlet
Letter, The House of the Seven Gables, The Blithedale Romance,* and *The Marble Faun.* He de-emphasized history and
the simple view of society in favor of a new and deep interest
in contemporary attitudes,[85] the universal questions of good
and evil, the effects of behavior on the psyche, especially in
The Scarlet Letter, and the shortsightedness of many reformers,
as revealed in *Mosses* and in the character of Hollingsworth.
The early sketches of *Twice-Told Tales* are filled with sentiment and are generally quite essaylike in style. Hawthorne
almost seems to be concerned with history for its own sake in
those stories. *Mosses,* although often presenting characters
who are mechanically drawn across the stages of the sketches
and allegories in "processional" fashion, does show Hawthorne's development in contriving situations aimed at illus-
trating the philosophic inadequacies of both the Transcendentalists and himself, retrospectively. In *The Scarlet Letter,*
Hawthorne moves away from the basically negative and satiric
thrust of *Mosses* to his own positive, albeit perhaps overemphasized, statement of the power of evil. Although there is an
element of anti-Transcendentalism in his treatment of Hester,
that element itself is finally lost in Hawthorne's overall philosophic position. He could empathize with Hester, but he could

not in good conscience provide her with an escape from the past. It is no small coincidence that *The Scarlet Letter* is both a statement of Hawthorne's own beliefs and his best work. All of these new concerns, evidenced as they are in his most important works, were brought about by Hawthorne's search for audience appeal and, more importantly, by the impact Transcendentalism had on him. Hawthorne always felt that *The Scarlet Letter* was a dark book, an overstatement. For that reason, *Blithedale*—a more objective review of Transcendentalism and reform, a distilled reaction—is the best work in which to investigate Hawthorne's attitudes toward Transcendentalism.

The Marble Faun attempts through a change in setting and a return to the past to put events in a direct line of descent from the fall itself and thus make the action and theme all the more powerful. Hawthorne tries to make the fall of Donatello a *felix culpa*, but the resolution of the book is puzzling and *The Marble Faun* becomes, finally, a prelude to artistic incapability rather than a greater artistic achievement for him. His career ended on May 19, 1864, after he tried unsuccessfully to complete another romance. He left behind four unfinished fragments: *The Ancestral Footstep, Dr. Grimshawe's Secret, Septimius Felton,* and *The Dolliver Romance.*[86]

CONCLUSION

THE spirit of Transcendentalism had an undeniably important effect on a large number of Salem's inhabitants. The problem of separating and assessing influences is, however, considerable, especially when one takes into account the organic nature of the movement. Transcendentalism changed the lives of people in Salem, and yet that influence is ultimately incapable of specific documentation. The growth of the lyceum movement and the emergence of Transcendentalism are inseparable phenomena and must be regarded as such by students of the period. Surprisingly, however, not nearly enough research has been done on the way these movements influenced one another or on the impact both of them had on small New England communities like Salem.

The lyceum movement and Transcendentalism, mainly through the great popularity of Emerson, brought about a great interest in learning and a concern for the quality of life. This popularity is attested to chiefly by the large audiences that attended lectures at the Salem Lyceum Hall. Hollow materialism in Salem, already suffering from a severe case of dry rot, was toppled by the flourish of an intellectualism that was unprecedented in our history. It was not a renaissance as such because America had never before experienced anything like it. The intellectual flowering was for that reason all the more startling. The political and social revolutions that had shaken France and this country a half century earlier were now ready for their intellectual, aesthetic, and spiritual counterparts.

Salem had its museums, libraries, newspapers, periodicals, musical societies, progressive schools, and famous citizens, many of whom graduated from Harvard. These cultural advantages were not enough however; the people hungered for something more to make them whole and they yearned for someone to show them how to live. They needed stimulation, leadership, and spiritual elevation. The lyceum touched everyone, cut across social strata and spanned all age groups, and it excited the people as no written word could have done. The lyceum was practical in all its concerns as well. Although what was taught in lyceum lectures would have to be revised and updated later, the universal but practical concerns of the conduct of life that Emerson taught would be long lasting.

Since Emerson's early and most significant lectures were delivered in Salem, as well as elsewhere, Salem was very early influenced by his thinking. Most scholars agree that Transcendentalism reached its peak during the decade 1836–46. From 1830 through 1836, however, Emerson, the Salem audience (particularly in 1836), and audiences wherever Emerson lectured helped to shape and direct the movement. In those early lectures Emerson crystallized his own view of Transcendentalism without the encumbrance, for himself or his audiences, of that particular label. He set forth his ideas and they were well received, but the lecturer-audience relationship was more complex. As Carl Bode has stressed, some of the world's greatest artistic masterpieces have come out of the heat of artist-patron friction.[1] One can readily find examples of this process in the visual arts, he says, but patronage of this nature is historically rare in literature. The writer has seldom if ever had his reader by his side to offer immediate responses. Yet such response was an essential feature of the lecturing process. There was no formal question-and-answer period following a lyceum lecture, but there was the heightened sensitivity of the lecturer to his audience to inform him of his success. For better or worse, the lecturer came away from the lecture knowing what had been said and what still had to be said, and also what had to be revised for the next performance or for publication. By submitting himself to the rigors and pressures of the lecture platform, the lecturer knew which ideas and expressions were unacceptable, which ideas sounded very unlike what he meant to say, and which ideas touched his audience favorably. An inherent feature of the lyceum was that the audience demanded the best from a lecturer. Although there was always the possibility of varying degrees of disinterest on the part of the audience, never before had the people of any country taken such an active part in the creation of their own literature. As already noted, Emerson was well aware of the need to give his audiences what they wanted, that is, what the times demanded, as well as to give them what he personally felt they needed, regardless of the consequences. His creativity and intellectual development seemed, finally, to thrive on the tensions created by this dual demand.

Transcendentalism through the lyceum brought into view a whole new side of life and helped to define a native but long dormant American idealism for the people of Salem. Emerson and all the Transcendentalists taught them how to live and what to live for, and they reacted favorably to the direction provided by this new philosophy. Salemites and the Transcendentalists worked together to define a new identity for the town and the whole country, and this new identity involved a much greater concern for culture, matters of the intellect, and the quality of life.

As a philosophic and literary movement that lasted for several decades, Transcendentalism had momentum and, as complex and diverse as it was, its forces were concentrated. The reaction against the movement never had such a definable shape. The opposing force, characterized mainly as emotional reflex actions, had two targets in Salem. The first of these was the attack on Jones Very by Upham and Brazer. This attack, which was directed at Very's eccentricity, was similar to attacks made against William Ellery Channing II, another Transcendental poet. Very was the kind of radical figure who not only attracted conservative reaction but also sought it out and provoked it. There is also some reason to believe that Upham as a minister was envious of the enthusiasm of the crowds who were drawn to the lyceum lectures. Upham had been instrumental in getting the lyceum started, and as a college friend of Emerson's he had invited Emerson to lecture in Salem. However, when Very began to act strangely on that September day in 1838, Upham placed all the blame on Emerson.

Upham's negative reaction to Transcendentalism, though important in the history of Salem, was personal to Upham and was not typical. Upham may have realized that he had made a mistake in entering the Unitarian ministry and, consequently, may have become annoyed by Emerson's successes. This idea is supported by several facts. Correspondence between the two men was early and brief, and Upham eventually left the church to enter politics and, later, to write history. Upham was obviously an ambitious man who had not really found his proper calling—a man who might have felt challenged by the intellectuals around him. He identified Elizabeth Peabody with Emerson and refused to associate with her; and, later, when Upham became a Whig leader in Salem, he used his influence to have Hawthorne dismissed from his post at the Custom House. Furthermore, since there is no evidence of any criticism of either Very or Emerson in the Salem newspapers on this matter, the nature of the argument seems to have been personal. The reaction of Brazer, who at least tried to question Very on religious grounds, may be judged to be more sincere and less of a personal attack.

Thus, Upham's reaction was against an eccentric, religious fanatic and was a conflict of personalities that was thinly disguised as philosophic and religious disagreement, a conflict between Transcendentalism and Unitarianism. Emerson's cool response to the whole affair was appropriate and was the one that history would take.

The second target of the reaction, by no means as colorful as the reaction to Very's behavior, concerned the rhetoric of the movement's spokesmen. One comment that was made in many a review of an Emerson lecture was that the lecture was impossible to summarize. Most reviewers, perhaps as enthralled by Emerson as the rest of the audience, found it impossible to take notes and listen to the lectures at the same time. The criticism that the seemingly essential principles that the Transcendentalists were attempting to convey should not be obfuscated by unwieldy rhetoric seems, in part, justified. However, when one realizes how the emotions were aroused by such rhetoric, that so much of the spirit of the movement was symbolized and conveyed by that rhetoric, it is difficult to see the rhetoric as a shortcoming. If a reviewer had difficulty in completely understanding the lecturer, one must not assume that the audience had not been reached to some degree, at least. Reviews that criticized the supposed obfuscatory rhetoric of the Transcendental lectures were naturally more common in the less cultured sections of the country. The attack by Nichols in his manuscript should be considered, in part, a comment by a foreigner on the ambitiousness of Salem's lyceum in offering Transcendental lectures to general audiences. The Salem audience, admittedly not to be compared to midwestern audiences, obviously believed that their money was well spent since they repeatedly invited Emerson and the other Transcendentalists to lecture in Salem.

In the final analysis, Very's troubles and the reaction to the rhetoric of Transcendentalism were but slight detractions from the many successes that Transcendentalism experienced in Salem. Emerson's lectures and Walker's lecture on Transcendentalism had taught the people of Salem and beyond just what this new philosophy was, and Walker's lecture, in particular, is as clear and intelligent a statement as can be found anywhere. The lecture by William Silsbee shows how much the philosophy was in the air at Harvard, and the occurrence of this lecture reveals how Transcendentalism had very quietly sprung up within the town of Salem. Silsbee remained a Unitarian minister all his life; he never became a Transcendentalist. There is every reason to believe, however, that the spirit of Transcendentalism had broadened his philosophy. All these influences and effects were important, but Salem's own contributions to the movement should not be diminished by comparison. Elizabeth Palmer Peabody was an independent and self-reliant woman who tried to bring Jones Very fully into the Transcendental group; and, although that attempt failed, one can readily see why it was made and why it did not succeed. In reviewing the matter of a native Transcendentalism, one cannot easily overlook the effects of the movement on Octavius B. Frothingham and his *Transcendentalism in New England* or on Very's former student Samuel Johnson, Jr. The particular manifestation of the new spirit in their works deserves its own special treatment as it belongs to a later period, which this investigation cannot reasonably encompass. Finally, when one considers the objections to the style and rhetoric of the philosophy, the Transcendentalists must be commended for their desire to uplift the spirit and their unwillingness to oversimplify or reduce their material to the lowest common denominator of their audiences. Their tasks were to teach and show the way, and these they accomplished admirably.

Many things need to be said about Hawthorne's relationship with the Transcendental group and Transcendentalism in general. His connections to the movement were varied and intimate. They began in the social sense with his wife and branched out to touch almost every major figure in the movement. Recent scholarship has suggested that Hawthorne may have felt more intensely about Jones Very, Bronson Alcott, and Henry David Thoreau than had previously been suspected, and that perhaps he felt less able to relate genuinely to Emerson.[2] This scholarship as well as earlier evidence has indicated that there were specific artistic influences between Thoreau and Hawthorne and maybe even between Very and Hawthorne.

It has long been taken for granted that Hawthorne's artistic concerns were in many ways related to the aesthetic concerns of the Transcendentalists. In dealing with the human heart, psychology, morals, ethics, and the very stuff of art, reality, dreams, and imagination, his writings are concerned with the great issues of any age and place. For these reasons, Herman Melville went so far as to see in Hawthorne the closest literary descendant of Shakespeare that America had produced up to that time.[3] Was Hawthorne then a Transcendentalist? Not in the particular sense, but insofar as Transcendentalism and the creation of fiction for Hawthorne touched upon some of the same problems and principles, there is a spiritual kinship evidenced between Transcendentalism and his work. Also, one cannot overlook Hawthorne's stay at Brook Farm or his three-year residence in Concord, the very center of New England Transcendentalism, which tie him to the movement.

The advent of the Transcendental movement served Hawthorne in some very essential ways as have been previously argued. Through the personalities of his wife and Elizabeth Peabody, the new spirit helped to lighten the burden of the past that Hawthorne carried. The geniality of Sophia Peabody, who later became his wife, and the assertiveness of Elizabeth Peabody helped to bring Hawthorne out of his physical and mental seclusion and caused him to examine his surroundings. Elizabeth Peabody also encouraged him as a writer. Hawthorne's own sense of the past, which was for him inseparable from Salem itself, could provide only so much in the form of artistic source material. Hawthorne must have sensed the weight of the past on him in Salem, as it contrasted with the spirit of Transcendentalism as it was manifested in the lyceum, his wife, Elizabeth Peabody, and Jones Very. Hawthorne went to Brook Farm to provide himself with a relatively unencumbered income, he thought, but one also gets the idea that Hawthorne knew important things were happening all around him, which could be the basis of artistic creation. His later residence in Concord was yet another move toward greater social and artistic involvement.

Out of Hawthorne's great sense of the weight of the past and his attempt to throw himself out of the "arched window" of the House of the Seven Gables into the crowd below, to become more involved in life, comes the friction of the Paul Pry figures, *Mosses*, and all of his novels. There is friction and tension in this attraction-repulsion syndrome, but there is also a philosophic friction that is tied more closely to Transcendentalism. Hawthorne showed considerable distaste for millennialism. He had a strong dislike for reform and reformers, those that were a part of the Transcendental movement as well as those that were erroneously linked to it. Furthermore, he could not understand why the Transcendentalists would not accept the fact that a "ruined wall" cannot be repaired, or that the question even mattered. These were the anti-romantic, anti-Transcendental attitudes and beliefs that produced the satirical allegories of *Mosses* and forced Hawthorne to end *The Scarlet Letter* the way he did. *The Scarlet Letter* may have been an overstatement but the more objectively worked out resolutions of his other major works make them less rather than more satisfying than *The Scarlet Letter*. In addition, the resolutions of his other works reflect how deeply embedded in his very being the major contradictory forces of his works were.

Nathaniel Hawthorne was one of the most independent thinkers in this period of American literature and he showed his self-reliance in everything he did and wrote. He was a Salemite, but grew to dislike the town and at least one of its leading citizens, Charles W. Upham in particular. Yet his ties to the town were strong and history has tended to make them appear even stronger. The ambivalence, the attraction and repulsion to life and social involvement, manifested in any of the Paul Pry figures, and in Hawthorne himself, may also be a reflection of Hawthorne's birthplace. The fact that Salem and Hawthorne both had a preoccupation with the past, but also yearned for the future, and that both became satiric in their own ways makes the comparison feasible. The particular brand of Transcendentalism of Jones Very and Elizabeth Peabody and their differences with the leading Transcendentalists also tend to support the idea that those connected with both Transcendentalism and Salem responded to the movement in unique and perhaps more conservative ways. Transcendentalism had enlivened Salem, and it might be argued that if this is true Hawthorne did not have to leave Salem to be either favorably affected by or critical of the movement. It is obvious, however, that while Brook Farm could be the basis of a long work the lyceum was hardly the raw material of fiction.

Transcendentalism provided Hawthorne with issues but it could not do the same for Salem. Philosophy, not projects, was the major manifestation of the movement in Salem and only in a very limited sense, if at all, could social relationships there be the basis of fiction. Brook Farm and Concord were exciting places where experience and, therefore, fiction might come a little easier. As an artist, Hawthorne knew that he had to become engaged in life and it was the spirit of a new philosophy in the air in Salem that led him out of Salem. Like the owls that he describes in *The House of the Seven Gables*, he could not, however, escape the penumbra of the past and come fully into the light of the present. Transcendentalism, more than any other single influence on him, was instrumental, however, in developing his philosophy, shaping his writings, and creating the tensions on which any artist thrives.

APPENDIX

ABSTRACT OF DR. WALKER'S LECTURE°

There are some words, said Mr Walker, which affect us by what they mean, and there are some which affect us by the multitude of associations and prejudices they call up in association with them. Of this latter class is the word *Transcendentalism*, a word which stands in many minds—not as a representative of a certain class of truths—but for all that is visionary, vague, and mystical. This is the more remarkable, in that the author of the system under this name was of all men the most removed from the indefinite in expression and thought. And his system was diametrically opposite in character to that confused mass of notions which goes in our community under the indefinite term, German metaphysics. It is true that Dugald Stuart, at the close of a long life devoted to metaphysical study, said that he could not understand the philosopher of Koenisburg;—and it may be asked if he could not, who can? The lecturer added—that however that might be, the *difficulty* was of a very different nature from what is generally understood to be; it did not resemble the difficulty of understanding Jacob Boehman, Emanuel Swedenborg, and theosophists in general; neither did it resemble the difficulty of Sartor Resartus; but it was a difficulty analogous to that of understanding the processes and truths of Pure Mathematics, and arising from an analogous source—as it mainly consisted in the power of attention it presupposed, requiring of the student or reader the labor of a constant and severe abstraction, in order to keeping before the mind the terms of *the transcendental problems*—a problem forced upon Kant by the scepti-

°The Salem *Gazette*, March 6, 1838.

cism of David Hume, and to which there has never been any answer given so clear and definite. Other difficulties also besides this essential one, have made Kant unintelligible to the English. His own countrymen complain of his involved style of expression, and his barbarous terminology. The latter however contributes to his clearness, when its force is once learnt. But perhaps the main difficulty for English readers is, that we are not familiar with the terms of the philosophy of Descartes, Malebranche, and Leibnitz, in which Kant was trained, and which moulded the language and associations of the German mind. Our philosophic language is very much like that of Locke, but neither Locke nor the French materialists ever made any impression in Germany. Hence we find ourselves among strangers, when we do not find ourselves among the terms of Locke's philosophy. On this account also, the epitomes of Kant made now and then in the English and American journals have given little light. Of Epitomes in general, it may be said that though very satisfactory to proficients, they generally prove but stumbling blocks to beginners who are ignorant of the very alphabet of the science. Nor as yet have any successful attempts been made to render the "critique of Pure Reason" into English. Its translators could translate the words, but not the ideas. An adequate translation is yet to be made.

We shall omit the agreeable memoir of Kant with which the lecturer now proceeded. It showed, (to use his own words) that Kant was no more of a mystic, or idealist highflyer, than Newton or Locke; that he was cold, severe, and logical, in his habits of mind; and simple, modest and retiring in character. One proof of the latter is too interesting to omit. Of the several thousand books written to develope, unfold, refute and apply to every branch of human knowledge the principles of the "Critique," he is said never to have read one except one in manuscript sent to him by a disciple and friend—who had run a parallel between Jesus Christ and Kant, on their moral systems. Kant returned the manuscript to his friend with the advice not to publish it, but at any rate, *charged him* not to allow the offensive parallel to remain. "Seeing that one of these names is that to which *the heavens bow*; while the other is only that of a poor scholar, striving at the best of his ability feebly to illustrate some of the doctrines of his Master." This acknowledgement of Christianity is the more valuable, in that he was not of that ardent temperament which is naturally pious, and is said to have been *slow* to admit the supernatural evidence of Christianity.

The lecturer next proceeded to state the circumstances of the philosophical world which gave rise to the transcendental problem.

John Locke, the great English philosopher, in his enquiry into the human understanding, had deduced all our knowledge from two classes of facts. External facts made known to us by the five senses, and Internal facts produced by the act of reflecting on our sensations. Both of these classes of facts he comprehended under the general name of Experience. Experience then is the only ground of human knowledge, according to Locke.

It never occurred to Mr Locke to ask himself, what made us capable of experience; what *legitimated* the ideas derived from experience; and this fatal oversight gave rise to that error of method which eventuated in the sceptical system of Hume and the materialism of the French.

So far was Mr Locke however from seeing these consequences, that the lecturer thought, had the controversies of his day, brought out this weak point of his analysis, he would have frankly acknowledged the error, and his searching mind gone deeper and found the truth. Even, as it was, he had stepped out of the right line of sensualism. For he had admitted internal facts produced by reflection. This indeed did not supply the deficiency in Hobbes' analysis, but it was turning away from it. It did not advance into spiritualism, but it was the entrance of the road to it.

David Hume's quick mind saw the consequences of Locke's theory, and carried it out into a system of scepticism unanswerable on the premises. He showed by a subtle analysis, (we will not attempt to follow the lecturer in his summary of this) that we are capable of experience only so far as we believe in the necesary connection of cause and effect. But a necessary idea cannot be derived from experience—we cannot derive from experience that which makes us capable of experience. And since, according to Mr Locke, we have no ideas save those we derive from experience, the necessary connection of cause and effect is an illusion, a figment of the brain, a nothing. On this figment, this illusion, this nothing, however, is all our knowledge based. Since there is no evidence of truth, no *philosophical* ground for belief!

Thus did Hume cut up under their feet the whole ground of belief for the philosophers of his day. The philosophy of Locke had no answer to return to this statement. The question now came, not whether this or that system is right; but can there be any philosophy whatever? The first answer to Hume was made by what is called the Scotch common sense school. Dr. Reid declared that Mr Locke's analysis was defective; that to the reflective faculty were presented not merely the facts of sensation, but another class of facts, original belief, laws of the mind itself, by the faculty of consciousness. I strike a table and look into my mind to see what is there in consequence. First is the sensation of the blow:—but there are also two other ideas—an idea of myself, and an idea of the external world. Where do these ideas come from? They are not involved in the sensation; they are not similar to it; they differ from it and from each other; the sensation is merely the occasion, not the cause of these other ideas. These ideas are not *innate* in the sense that they are in the mind before they spring up there; but they inevitably and universally spring up in the mind, by an original law, which is essentially independent of the senses. As the sound of a coach, does, after certain experiences, suggest the picture and idea of a coach, which has no resemblance to the sound; so are *natural suggestions* made: so the touch of my hand to the table suggests the idea of myself, and the idea of an external world. This class of truths, not referable to sensation, but to another faculty or element of the mind, is *transcendentalism. Transcendentalism* is the answer to the universal scepticism of Hume. It is sometimes called the *a priori* element of human intelligence. The mind supplies it to reflection. It *transcends* experience; it is that in human intelligence which makes us capable of experience. Hume was answered not by breaking the meshes of his reasoning, but by going up to his premises, and supplying the deficiency there, which was originally produced by Locke's defective analysis.

But what did *Kant* do? The German philosopher published the "critique of Pure Reason," seventeen years after Dr. Reid. The lecturer did not say whether Kant knew of Reid's system, but merely that Kant, by a route entirely his own and perfectly original; by the nicest analysis and severest logic; came to the same truth, and stated it a thousandfold more scientifically and clearly. The Scotch school had left the transcendental element quite undefined. Their "first principles" were now few, and now multiplied, as by Lord Kaimes indefinitely. Some advantages attend leaving the subject thus at loose ends, for we are not yet prepared, perhaps to systematise so rigorously as Kant has done; we have not yet the materials for a perfect system. Kant's method however makes whatever he did discover more available as an instrument. He undertook to state precisely what the mind supplied to experience, and what sensation supplied. By sensation, he said, the raw material of nature is supplied. The raw material is various. Hence the Variable element of human knowledge. The mind, on the other hand, is alone *formative*, it consists of *moulds*, into which the raw materials of nature flow and are stamped. Hence the *invariable* element of human knowledge. Nor did the philosopher stop here. He undertook to number and name *categoaries*, and hence the celebrated *transcendental table*. We understood from the lecturer that the work on Pure Reason is the explanation and justification of these several categories. He did not speak at all of the works on the Practical Reason, and on Religion, which followed some years after.

Having, (with a felicity of expression, we have not been able to follow with our abstract,) thus shown us what transcendentalism, strictly speaking, is, Mr Walker proceeded to speak of its uses. Its first use was its answer to Hume. A more permanent use is to be found in its bearings on the questions of Expediency and Fatalism. These questions have arisen out of a want of a philosophical statement of the *transcendental* or *a priori* element of human intelligence, which Kant supplies. In all times the transcendental doctrine has been believed *practically*. In all languages are words corresponding to our words *ought* and *will*, which correspond to the ideas of Right and Freedom and prove that these ideas have always been recognised practically. Yet it is much to have a philosophical ground provided for them. Thus alone can the spread of mysticism be checked. He then intimated that there were mystics in our day, who proposed unconsidered impulse instead of considered principle, at the guide of action. Their existence proved the craving of human nature for something beyond an empirical philosophy. These are signs of the times, and their enthusiasm, kindled at a divine source, may not be quenched. It must be met and satisfied; by accepting and defining that in human intelligence of which it dreams; and which is what gives life to all true virtue, and all enduring worship.

But we regret of an attempt to speak of this last paragraph. It was sublime, notwithstanding the quotation from Scaliger, which foolish in its first application, was singularly inconclusive here, and even told the contrary way, in the lecturer's application of it to the Poetic school of Philosophers.

NOTES

INTRODUCTION

1. Bliss Perry, "The Centenary of Hawthorne," *Atlantic* 94 (August 1904), 195–206.

2. Frank P. Stearns, *The Life and Genius of Nathaniel Hawthorne* (Philadelphia, 1906), p. 197.

3. Ibid., p. 196.

4. Ibid., p. 199.

5. John Erskine, "Hawthorne," *The Cambridge History of American Literature*, ed. William P. Trent et al., vol. 2 (New York, 1918), p. 17.

6. Henry Seidel Canby, *Classic Americans: A Study of Eminent American Writers From Irving to Whitman* (New York, 1931), p. 231.

7. Austin Warren, ed., *Nathaniel Hawthorne: Representative Selections* (New York, 1934), pp. xl–xlvii.

8. F. O. Matthiessen, *American Renaissance: Art and Expression in the Age of Emerson and Whitman* (New York, 1941), pp. 179–368 *passim*.

9. For an evaluation of Hawthorne's attitude concerning reform, see Lawrence S. Hall, *Hawthorne: Critic of Society* (New Haven, 1944), pp. 8–31; Roy R. Male, *Hawthorne's Tragic Vision* (Austin, Tex., 1957), pp. 35–37; and Hyatt Howe Waggoner, *Hawthorne: A Critical Study*, rev. ed. (Cambridge, Mass., 1963), pp. 13–23.

10. Floyd Stovall, *American Idealism* (1943; reissued Port Washington, N.Y., 1965), pp. 63–67.

11. Millicent Bell, *Hawthorne's View of the Artist* (New York, 1962), pp. 12–15, 32–34.

12. Marjorie Elder, *Nathaniel Hawthorne: Transcendental Symbolist* (Athens, Ohio, 1969), pp. 3–4, 171–72.

13. Milton R. Stern, "American Values and Romantic Fiction," in *American Fiction: Historical and Critical Essays*, ed. James Nagel (Boston, 1977), pp. 13–33.

14. See my note 3, Chapter 4 for quotations from Stern.

15. Waggoner, *Hawthorne*, p. 3.

16. *The Complete Works of Ralph Waldo Emerson*, Centenary Edition, ed. Edward Waldo Emerson, 12 vols. (Boston and New York, 1903–04), 1:3.

CHAPTER 1: SALEM IN 1830

1. Charles Osgood and H. M. Batchelder, "Salem," *Standard History of Essex*

County, Massachusetts, comp. Cyrus Mason Tracy, William E. Graves, and Henry M. Batchelder (Boston, 1878), p. 360. See also Joseph B. Felt, *Annals of Salem* (Salem and Boston, 1849), hereafter cited as *Annals.* I have relied almost solely upon Felt's comprehensive records for information concerning Salem in 1830.

2. Samuel Eliot Morison, *The Maritime History of Massachusetts: 1783–1860* (Boston, 1921), pp. 79–95. Morison devotes an entire chapter, "The Salem East Indies," to the importance of Salem to the sea trade of Massachusetts. This chapter, which views the earlier period of 1790–1812, provides a good historical background, however, for the period discussed here.

3. John Warner Barber, *Massachusetts Towns: An 1840 View* (2nd ed., 1840; reprint ed., Barre, Mass., 1963), p. 100.

4. Morison, *Maritime History,* pp. 213–24.

5. For a more detailed analysis of the extent of Salem's shipping, see the tonnage chart in Morison, *Maritime History,* p. 378.

6. *Annals,* 2:411.

7. Ibid., p. 440.

8. Ibid., pp. 430–31.

9. Ibid., p. 421.

10. Ibid., p. 422.

11. For a fuller discussion of the literary figures who lived in Salem until the twentieth century, see John W. Buckham, "Literary Salem," *Essex Institute Historical Collections* 63 (July 1907):193–98.

12. Louise Hall Tharp, *The Peabody Sisters of Salem* (Boston, 1950), p. 43.

13. *Annals,* 2:403.

14. Ibid., pp. 402–8.

15. Ibid., p. 207.

16. Ibid., p. 180.

17. Ibid.

18. Morison, *Maritime History,* p. 109.

19. *Annals,* 2:171.

20. Ibid., p. 183.

21. Ibid., pp. 162–63.

22. Robert Greenhalgh Albion, "From Sails to Spindles: Essex County in Transition," *Essex Institute Historical Collections* 95 (April 1959):115–36.

23. Osgood and Batchelder, "Salem," p. 380.

24. Ibid.

25. Ibid.

26. *Annals,* 2:30–37.

27. Ibid., p. 35.

28. Ibid., p. 33.

29. Harriet Silvester Tapley, *Salem Imprints: 1768–1825* (Salem, 1927), pp. 3–4.

30. *Annals,* 2:12–13.

31. Ibid., pp. 14–23.

32. Ibid., p. 39.

33. Ibid., pp. 38–39.

34. Ibid., pp. 40–41. See also Carl Bode, *The American Lyceum: Town Meeting of the Mind* (New York, 1956).

35. *Annals*, 2:71.

36. Robert Cantwell, *Nathaniel Hawthorne: The American Years* (New York, 1948), p. 148.

37. *Annals*, 2:80–81. See also Frederic Alan Sharf, "Charles Osgood: The Life and Times of a Salem Portrait Painter," *Essex Institute Historical Collections* 102 (July 1966):203–12.

38. This painting is in the Essex Institute.

39. *Annals*, 2:84. See also Morison, *Maritime History*, pp. 119–21 and the special Samuel McIntire issue of *Essex Institute Historical Collections* 93 (April–July 1957).

40. Morison, *Maritime History*, p. 121.

41. *Annals*, 2:90.

42. *Constitution of the Mozart Association, Instituted in Salem, June, 1825* (Salem, 1826) in the Essex Institute.

43. *Annals*, 2:44.

44. Ibid., pp. 44–45.

45. Ibid., pp. 84–98.

46. Ibid., p. 95.

47. Ibid., p. 93.

48. Cantwell, *Nathaniel Hawthorne*, p. 112.

49. Ibid., p. 151.

50. Ibid., p. 152.

51. Ibid., p. 153.

52. *Annals*, 2:465–67.

53. Cantwell, *Nathaniel Hawthorne*, p. 160.

CHAPTER 2: TRANSCENDENTALISM IN SALEM

1. Carl Bode, *The American Lyceum: Town Meeting of the Mind* (New York, 1956), pp. 46–49 *passim*.

2. "The American Lyceum," *Old South Leaflets*, vol. 6, no. 139 (Boston, n.d.), pp. 293–305.

3. Charles W. Upham, "A Circular Letter Issued Pursuant to the Vote of a Convention Held at Topsfield, Dec. 30, 1829, for Establishing a County Lyceum," *Essex Institute Historical Collections* 18 (December 1881):293–306.

4. Upham, "A Circular Letter," p. 301.

5. The Salem *Gazette*, January 19, 1830.

6. Ibid., February 23, 1830.

7. John A. Pollard, "Lyceum Lectures Drew Brilliant Minds to Salem," *Salem Evening News*, December 12, 1929. Henry K. Oliver in the *Historical Sketch of the Salem Lyceum with a list of the Officers and Lectures Since its formation in 1830 and an extract from the address of Gen. Henry K. Oliver delivered at the Opening of the Fiftieth Annual Course of Lectures Nov. 13, 1878* (Salem, 1879) more authoritatively gives the cost of the hall as $3036.76 and the land as $750.00. See also Robert Samuel Rantoul, "Story of Old Lyceum Hall," *Salem Evening News*, March 5, 1915. The floor plan for Lyceum Hall is in the Essex Institute's Salem Lyceum Collection.

8. *The American Lyceum: Its History and Contribution to Education*, U.S. Department of Interior Bulletin No. 12 (Washington, D.C.: Government Printing Office, 1942), p. 42.

9. *The American Lyceum: Its History and Contribution to Education*, p. 10.

10. Minutes of the Salem Lyceum meetings in the Essex Institute.

11. *The Journals and Miscellaneous Notebooks of Ralph Waldo Emerson*, ed. William H. Gilman et al., vol. 5 (1835–38), ed. Merton M. Sealts, Jr. (Cambridge, Mass., 1965), p. 376, hereafter cited as *JMN*.

12. Oliver, *Historical Sketch*, p. 41.

13. William D. Dennis, "The Salem Charitable Mechanic Association," *Essex Institute Historical Collections* 42 (January 1906):15. The Salem Lyceum actually held shares in the Salem Mechanic Association.

14. Entry dated October 1, 1851, in the unpublished diary of Susan Louise Waters in the Essex Institute Diary Collection.

15. Pollard, "Lyceum Lectures."

16. Waters, Diary (unpaginated).

17. See the Salem *Gazette* for March 25, 1831, February 14, 1840, and December 4, 1846. In a broadside dated October 1840, the Salem Lyceum published a series of resolutions that had been passed to deal with the problem of rowdyism.

18. *The Correspondence of Henry David Thoreau*, ed. Walter Harding and Carl Bode (New York, 1958), pp. 233–34, hereafter cited as *Correspondence*.

19. Oliver, *Historical Sketch, passim*.

20. Ibid., pp. 54–55.

21. Pollard, "Lyceum Lectures."

22. Ibid.

23. See Herbert A. Wichelns, "Ralph Waldo Emerson," *A History and Criticism of American Public Address*, ed. William Norwood Brigance, vol. 2 (New York, 1943), pp. 501–25.

24. Cited by David Mead, *Yankee Eloquence in the Middle West: The Ohio Lyceum 1850–1870* (East Lansing, Mich., 1951), pp. 42–43.

25. Untitled, undated newspaper clipping in the 1860 Almanac Diary of Asa Lamson in the Essex Institute Diary Collection.

26. *JMN*, vol. 4 (1832–34), ed. Alfred R. Ferguson (Cambridge, Mass., 1964), p. 372.

27. Ralph L. Rusk, *The Life of Ralph Waldo Emerson* (New York, 1949), p. 200.

28. *The Letters of Ralph Waldo Emerson*, ed. Ralph L. Rusk (New York, 1939), 1:397, hereafter cited as *Letters*.

29. Rusk, *The Life of Ralph Waldo Emerson*, p. 205.

30. *The Correspondence of Emerson and Carlyle*, ed. Joseph Slater (New York, 1964), p. 124.

31. Ibid.

32. "The Rage for Lectures," The Salem *Gazette*, March 14, 1943.

33. Information for this list of lectures is gathered chiefly from Oliver's *Historical Sketch*, William Charvat's *Emerson's American Lecture Engagements: A Chronological List* (New York, 1961), The Salem *Observer*, and The Salem *Gazette*. I have followed here Charvat's pattern of placing question marks before the dates of unsubstantiated appearances and after dates where the lecture was given and

the date is questionable.

34. *The Early Lectures of Ralph Waldo Emerson*, ed. Stephen E. Whicher and Robert E. Spiller, vol. 1 (Cambridge, Mass., 1959), p. 24, hereafter cited as *Early Lectures*.

35. *JMN*, 4:322.

36. *Early Lectures*, 1:110.

37. *Letters*, 2:9.

38. The Salem *Observer*, April 23, 1836.

39. Octavius B. Frothingham, *Transcendentalism in New England: A History* (1876; reprint ed., New York, 1959), pp. 120–21.

40. See Odell Shepard, *Pedlar's Progress: The Life of Bronson Alcott* (Boston, 1937), pp. 247–48.

41. Letter of February 26, 1838, from Elizabeth Palmer Peabody to Robert C. Waterston in the Essex Institute Autograph Collection.

42. The Salem *Gazette*, March 2, 1838.

43. See Alfred F. Rosa, ed., " 'Aesthetic Culture': A Lyceum Lecture by William Silsbee," *Essex Institute Historical Collections* 107 (January 1971):35–61, hereafter cited as " 'Aesthetic Culture.' "

44. " 'Aesthetic Culture,' " p. 38.

45. Ibid., pp. 39–40.

46. *Journals of Ralph Waldo Emerson*, ed. Edward Waldo Emerson and Waldo Emerson Forbes, 10 vols. (Boston and New York, 1909–14), 5:72–74.

47. Octavius B. Frothingham, *Theodore Parker: A Biography* (Boston, 1874), pp. 99–103.

48. Letter of September 24, 1838, from Elizabeth Palmer Peabody to Ralph Waldo Emerson in the Essex Institute Autograph Collection.

49. *Correspondence*, pp. 230–31.

50. The Salem *Observer*, November 4, 1848.

51. Ibid., November 25, 1848.

52. Oliver, *Historical Sketch*, p. 50.

53. J. Lyndon Shanley, *The Making of Walden, with the Text of the First Version* (Chicago, 1957) presents a thorough discussion of the composition of *Walden* but the lecture version is not extant and therefore not included.

54. Rose Hawthorne Lathrop, *Memories of Hawthorne* (London, 1897), pp. 92–93.

55. Oliver, *Historical Sketch*, p. 50.

56. *Correspondence*, pp. 233–34.

57. The Salem *Observer*, March 3, 1849.

58. Oliver, *Historical Sketch, passim*.

59. This date is calculated from the date of the review in the Salem *Observer*. Although the manuscript of this lecture is not available, it is clear from the contents of this review that it was the essay "Transcendentalism" or some version of it in *Theodore Parker: An Anthology*, ed. Henry Steele Commager (Boston, 1960), pp. 89–108. The references that follow are to this text and hereafter are cited as "Transcendentalism."

60. Parker, "Transcendentalism," p. 92.

61. Ibid., p. 93.

62. Ibid.

63. Ibid., p. 95.

64. The Salem *Observer*, January 13, 1849.

65. Oliver, *Historical Sketch, passim*.

66. Lathrop, *Memories of Hawthorne*, p. 92.

67. Octavius B. Frothingham, *Recollections and Impressions: 1822–1890* (New York, 1891), pp. 51–52.

68. Carl Bode, "The Sound of American Literature a Century Ago," *Proceedings of the British Academy* 47 (1961):102.

69. Henry Seidel Canby, *Thoreau* (Boston, 1939), p. 137. See also Walter Harding, *The Days of Henry Thoreau* (New York, 1966), pp. 235–42.

70. Merton M. Sealts, Jr., and Alfred R. Ferguson, eds., *Emerson's 'Nature'—Origin, Growth, Meaning* (New York, 1969), pp. 65–66.

71. The Salem *Observer*, June 3, 1848.

72. *Early Lectures*, 1:173.

73. See Louise Hall Tharp, *The Peabody Sisters of Salem* (Boston, 1950), *passim* and Gladys Brooks, *Three Wise Virgins* (New York, 1957), pp. 83–153.

74. Tharp, *The Peabody Sisters of Salem*, p. 27.

75. Ibid., p. 25.

76. *JMN*, vol. 3 (1826–32), ed. William H. Gilman and Alfred R. Ferguson (Cambridge, Mass., 1963), p. 282.

77. For a discussion of the similarities in the educational philosophies of Bronson Alcott and Maria Montessori, see Alfred F. Rosa, "Alcott and Montessori," *Connecticut Review* 3 (October 1969):98–103.

78. Hubert H. Hoeltje, *Inward Sky: The Mind and Heart of Nathaniel Hawthorne* (Durham, N.C., 1962), p. 142.

79. Notice of this lecture appeared in the Salem *Observer* on December 23, 1837. Information concerning Elizabeth's reaction to Very's lecture and her first meeting with him appears in Edwin Gittleman's *Jones Very: The Effective Years, 1833–1840* (New York, 1967), pp. 158–60. See also William Irving Bartlett, *Jones Very: Emerson's "Brave Saint"* (Durham, N.C., 1942), pp. 40–50.

80. Gittleman, *Jones Very*, p. 159.

81. Ibid., p. 160.

82. Ibid., p. 4.

83. Ibid., p. 7.

84. Ibid., pp. 12–13.

85. Ibid.

86. Ibid., p. 13.

87. Bartlett, *Jones Very*, p. 22.

88. Ralph Waldo Emerson, "New Poetry," *The Dial: A Magazine for Literature, Philosophy, and Religion*, vol. 1 (New York, 1961), pp. 221–22.

89. Bartlett, *Jones Very*, p. 26.

90. Ibid., p. 32.

91. Ibid., p. 35.

92. Gittleman, *Jones Very*, p. 186.

93. Ibid., p. 187.

94. Bartlett, *Jones Very*, p. 53.

95. See Carlos Baker, "Emerson and Jones Very," *New England Quarterly* 7

(March 1934):90–99; Yvor Winters, "Jones Very and R. W. Emerson," *Maule's Curse* (Norfolk, Conn., 1938), pp. 125–46; and Warner B. Berthoff, "Jones Very: New England Mystic," *Boston Public Library Quarterly* 2 (January 1950):63–76.

96. Nathan Lyons, ed., *Jones Very: Selected Poems* (New Brunswick, N.J., 1966), p. 10.

CHAPTER 3: SALEM'S REACTION TO TRANSCENDENTALISM

1. There has been no comprehensive study of the reaction to Transcendentalism. See Octavius B. Frothingham, *Transcendentalism in New England: A History* (1876; reprint ed., New York, 1959), pp. 137–41; Andrews Norton, "A Discourse on the Latest Form of Infidelity," and Orestes A. Brownson, "Transcendentalism," in *Selected Writings of the American Transcendentalists*, ed. George Hochfield (New York, 1966), pp. 203–9, 399–407; and Henry David Gray, *Emerson: A Statement of New England Transcendentalism as Expressed in the Philosophy of Its Chief Exponent* (1917; reprint ed., New York, 1965), pp. 7–17.

2. *The Letters of Ralph Waldo Emerson*, ed. Ralph L. Rusk, vol. 4 (New York, 1939), pp. 272–73.

3. Jonathan P. Nichols, Jr., "Lecture Delivered Before the Society of O. A." Unpublished manuscript in the Gilbert Streeter Collection in the Essex Institute.

4. Henry K. Oliver, *Historical Sketch of the Salem Lyceum with a list of the Officers and Lectures Since its formation in 1830 and an extract from the address of Gen. Henry K. Oliver delivered at the Opening of the Fiftieth Annual Course of Lectures* Nov. 13, 1878 (Salem, 1879), pp. 25–27.

5. For a discussion of this incident and other considerations in the composition of *The Scarlet Letter*, see Hubert H. Hoeltje, "The Writing of *The Scarlet Letter*," *New England Quarterly* 27 (September 1954):326–46.

6. *The Complete Works of Nathaniel Hawthorne, with Introductory Notes*, Riverside ed., ed. George P. Lathrop, 12 vols. (Boston, 1883), 5:43, hereafter cited as *Complete Works*.

7. Julian Hawthorne, *Nathaniel Hawthorne and His Wife: A Biography*, vol. 1 (Boston, 1885), pp. 443–47.

8. Ibid., p. 444.

9. For a discussion of the critical responses to *The Blithedale Romance*, see Bertha Faust, *Hawthorne's Contemporaneous Reputation: A Study of Literary Opinion in America and England, 1828–1864* (1939; reprint ed., New York, 1968), pp. 98–108.

10. For a full treatment of these events, see Edwin Gittleman, "Crisis-Comedy in Salem," *Jones Very: The Effective Years, 1833–1840* (New York, 1967), pp. 215–31 and William R. Hutchison, *The Transcendentalist Ministers: Church Reform in the New England Renaissance* (New Haven, 1959), p. 63.

11. For a brief sketch, see Randall Stewart, "Charles W. Upham," *Dictionary of American Biography*, 20 vols. (New York, 1928–40), 19:121–22. Upham was immortalized as Judge Pyncheon in Hawthorne's *The House of the Seven Gables* in reprisal for Hawthorne's dismissal from the Custom House, which Hawthorne thought to be chiefly the work of Upham.

12. Kenneth W. Cameron, *Emerson the Essayist*, vol. 1 (Hartford, Conn., 1945), p. 443.

13. Hutchison, *The Transcendentalist Ministers*, p. 63. For the best discussion of the miracles question, see Hutchison, pp. 52–97.

14. Merle E. Curti, "John Brazer," *Dictionary of American Biography*, 2:612–13.

15. A copy of Brazer's Dudleian Lecture *Review of the Argument in Support of Natural Religion* (Cambridge, Mass., 1835) is in the Essex Institute.

16. Curti, *Dictionary of American Biography*, 2:612–13.

17. Hutchison, *The Transcendentalist Ministers*, pp. 63–64, n. 23, comes to the same conclusion but offers no evidence for his correction of Curti's entry on Brazer.

18. Hutchison, *The Transcendentalist Ministers*, p. 63.

19. Cited by Gittleman, *Jones Very*, p. 219.

20. This remark, as well as the one by Elizabeth Peabody that refers to Brazer as a "ninny," puts Brazer in an unfavorable light; he seems not to have been very well liked or highly thought of. Additional support of this view is found in the November 1, 1840, diary entry of the intellectual Mary Pickman in the Essex Institute Diary Collection: "Mr. Brazer preached in the morn, on our Savior's example of considerateness. The sermon would have been quite a good one, but comeing [sic] from him spoiled it."

21. Letter of October 20, 1838, from Elizabeth Palmer Peabody to Ralph Waldo Emerson in the Essex Institute Autograph Collection.

22. Gittleman, *Jones Very*, p. 235.

23. See Julian Hawthorne, *Hawthorne and His Wife*, 1:166–67 and Robert Cantwell, *Nathaniel Hawthorne: The American Years* (New York, 1948), p. 472, n. 69.

24. Hubert H. Hoeltje, *Inward Sky: The Mind and Heart of Nathaniel Hawthorne* (Durham, N.C., 1962), p. 142.

25. Ibid., p. 144.

26. Ibid., p. 145.

27. Gittleman, *Jones Very*, p. 161.

28. Ibid., p. 282.

29. Letter of December 3, 1838, from Elizabeth Palmer Peabody to Ralph Waldo Emerson in the Essex Institute Autograph Collection.

30. Gittleman, *Jones Very*, p. 283.

31. See Cantwell, *Nathaniel Hawthorne*, p. 160 concerning the suspicion that surrounded the White murder case. Vernon Loggins, in *The Hawthornes* (New York, 1951), p. 239, goes as far as to say that Salem's economic change was precipitated by the White murder.

32. Gittleman, *Jones Very*, p. 284.

33. Robert D. Arner, "Hawthorne and Jones Very: Two Dimensions of Satire in 'Egotism; or, The Bosom Serpent,'" *New England Quarterly* 42 (June 1969):275.

34. *Love Letters of Nathaniel Hawthorne, 1839–41 and 1841–63*, vol. 1 (Chicago, 1907), p. 103.

35. *Complete Works*, 2:42.

36. Mark Van Doren, *Nathaniel Hawthorne* (New York, 1949), p. 123.

37. See Randall Stewart, "Hawthorne and Politics: Unpublished Letters to William B. Pike," *New England Quarterly* 5 (April 1932):237–63 and his *Nathaniel Hawthorne*:

A *Biography* (New Haven, 1948); Neal F. Doubleday, "Hawthorne's Criticism of New England Life," *College English* 2 (April 1941):639–53 and his "Hawthorne's Satirical Allegory," *College English* 3 (January 1942):325–37; Arlin Turner, "Hawthorne and Reform," *New England Quarterly* 15 (December 1942):700–714; and Lawrence S. Hall, *Hawthorne: Critic of Society* (New York, 1944). B. Bernard Cohen, in "Emerson's 'The Young American' and Hawthorne's 'The Intelligence Office,' " *American Literature* 26 (March 1954):32–43, has offered support for the view that there was mutual influence in his discussion of the term "Intelligence Office" in both those works. He argues that the two men had in their intense conversations some influence on each other.

38. Hoeltje, *Inward Sky*, pp. 212–13.

39. Ibid., p. 213. Emerson's attitude toward fiction in general is discussed thoroughly by John T. Flanagan, "Emerson as a Critic of Fiction," *Philological Quarterly* 15 (January 1936):30–45. Flanagan shows Emerson to have had a greater interest in fiction than had hitherto been believed but to be critically shortsighted in his excessive reliance on morality, most likely a remnant of Puritanism.

40. *The Correspondence of Henry David Thoreau*, ed. Walter Harding and Carl Bode (New York, 1958), p. 118.

41. *Complete Works*, 2:224.

42. Ibid., 3:432–33.

43. Hoeltje, *Inward Sky*, p. 208.

44. Nathaniel Hawthorne, *The American Notebooks*, ed. Randall Stewart (New Haven, 1932), p. 176, hereafter cited as *American Notebooks*.

45. Terence Martin, *Nathaniel Hawthorne* (New York, 1965), p. 181, n. 5.

46. This meeting is described by Hawthorne in *American Notebooks*, p. 160. Frank P. Stearns, in his *The Life and Genius of Nathaniel Hawthorne* (Philadelphia, 1906), p. 194, conjectures that the book Margaret Fuller carried was Kant's *Critique of Pure Reason*.

CHAPTER 4: NATHANIEL HAWTHORNE

1. John Erskine, "Hawthorne," *The Cambridge History of American Literature*, ed. William P. Trent et al., vol. 2 (New York, 1918), p. 16.

2. Henry Seidel Canby, *Classic Americans: A Study of Eminent American Writers from Irving to Whitman* (New York, 1931), p. 231.

3. *The Complete Works of Nathaniel Hawthorne, with Introductory Notes*, Riverside ed., ed. George P. Lathrop, 12 vols. (Boston, 1883), 2:107, hereafter cited as *Complete Works*. The most informed and provocative attempt to clarify the dilemma that Hawthorne felt uniquely victimized by is Milton R. Stern's "American Values and Romantic Fiction," in *American Fiction*, ed. James Nagel (Boston, 1977), pp. 13–33. The following is Stern's opening statement:

> One generally assumes that the driving impulse of American Romantic literature is the energy of Emersonian millennialism. In large measure this is true, especially for the earlier productions of Thoreau, Whitman, and Emerson himself. However, by suggesting some relationships between three of the commonplaces of twentieth-century criticism and scholarship, I wish to propose that

the center of energy in American Romantic fiction is not so much American millennialism as it is a creative set of recoils, or antagonisms, or tensions between the radicalism of millennial assumptions and a conservative, experiential response. (P. 13)

Stern sees the problems Hawthorne described as not unique to Hawthorne but common to all serious artists of the period:

In short, I propose the intricate irony of what appears to me to be a central fact of American Romantic fiction: in adopting the disguises of romance in order to express their recoil from their society's dearest assumptions, the American writers of serious Romantic fiction adopted a vocationally radical identity in order to express a philosophical conservatism that was at odds with the millennialistic assertions of American social conservatism, and that it is this irony that lies at the center of the tension within the selves of our serious Romantic fictionists, who, like Cooper, Poe, Hawthorne and Melville, yearned to belong to the common life, yearned to belong to the world of popular literary success, and who yet felt psychologically and vocationally alienated from what they yearned for. (P. 25)

And Stern continues:

My thesis is that whatever the idiosyncratic, creative, psychological centers of our writers' lives were, the common, cultural, creative, center of their lives was what really is a deeply political act: their attempt to mediate between the truth they wanted to tell their society and their society's unexamined assumptions. It was their attempt to mediate between their vocational and social identities, a conflict destructive of self and creative of fiction, and most intricately and dramatically seen in Hawthorne. In fact the generative cultural center of American literary creative vigor from Emerson on is a continuing dynamism of counter-impulsions toward and away from the millennialistic vision of possibilities so characteristic of American society. I think that in large outline, the fiction of the four major writers I have chosen, chosen because they are so major and so disparate, is in each case a complex and profoundly instructive history of the conflict. Another way of stating the proposition is that our greatest fiction writers of the Romantic period were, like Poe, so romantically transcendental that they repudiated the actualities, or, like Cooper, Hawthorne, and Melville, they were philosophically anti-Romantic. (Pp. 25–26)

The essay is filled with useful insights regarding the tensions that produced some of our best literature and should be read by all those interested in this period of our literature.

4. *Complete Works*, 2:224.
5. Ibid., pp. 246–47.
6. Ibid., 9:20–21.
7. Ibid., 2:50.
8. Ibid., p. 69.
9. Ibid.
10. Ibid., p. 196.
11. Ibid., p. 197.
12. Ibid., p. 201.
13. Ibid., p. 203.
14. Harold P. Miller, "Hawthorne Surveys His Contemporaries," *American Literature* 12 (May 1940):228–35.

15. Ibid., p. 230.

16. Ibid., p. 231.

17. Ibid.

18. Ibid. Additional support for the fact that Hawthorne is talking here about Emerson is the similarity in wording to a reference to Emerson in Hawthorne's *The American Notebooks*, ed. Randall Stewart (New Haven, 1932), p. 157, hereafter cited as *American Notebooks*.

19. Miller, "Hawthorne Surveys His Contemporaries," pp. 234–35.

20. Ibid., p. 235.

21. Ibid.

22. Buford Jones, " 'The Hall of Fantasy' and the Early Hawthorne-Thoreau Relationship," *PMLA* 83 (October 1968):1429–38. See also Frank Davidson, "Thoreau's Contributions to Hawthorne's *Mosses*," *New England Quarterly* 20 (December 1947):535–42; G. Thomas Couser, " 'The Old Manse,' *Walden*, and the Hawthorne-Thoreau Relationship," *ESQ* 21 (1st Quarter 1975):11–21; and R. W. B. Lewis, *The American Adam: Innocence, Tragedy, and Tradition in the Nineteenth Century* (Chicago, 1955), pp. 14–15.

23. *American Notebooks*, p. 167.

24. Jones, "Hawthorne-Thoreau Relationship," p. 1436.

25. Hyatt Howe Waggoner, *Hawthorne: A Critical Study*, rev. ed. (Cambridge, Mass., 1963), p. 4. For a discussion of how Hawthorne derived the name Gervayse Hastings from one of his ancestors, see Waggoner, p. 229.

26. *Complete Works*, 2:322.

27. Ibid., pp. 341–42.

28. Ibid., p. 342.

29. Ibid., p. 346.

30. Hubert H. Hoeltje, *Inward Sky: The Mind and Heart of Nathaniel Hawthorne* (Durham, N.C., 1962), pp. 238–39.

31. *Complete Works*, 2:147.

32. Ibid., p. 70.

33. Ibid., p. 78.

34. Ibid.

35. Ibid., p. 79.

36. Ibid., p. 85.

37. Ibid., pp. 87–88.

38. Ibid., pp. 432–33.

39. Ibid., pp. 438–39.

40. Ibid., p. 448.

41. Ibid., p. 449.

42. Ibid., pp. 443–44.

43. Ibid., p. 455.

44. Ibid., pp. 455–56.

45. Ibid., 5:67.

46. Ibid., p. 589.

47. See Waggoner, "The Scarlet Letter," *Hawthorne*, pp. 126–59 for a discussion of the imagery and characterization in *The Scarlet Letter*.

48. Moncure D. Conway, *Life of Nathaniel Hawthorne* (London, 1870); John

Erskine, "Hawthorne," *The Cambridge History of American Literature*, ed. William P. Trent et al., vol. 2 (New York, 1918), pp. 16–31; and Stuart P. Sherman, "Hawthorne," *Americans* (New York, 1922), pp. 122–52 have suggested a Transcendental viewpoint regarding Hester's and Dimmesdale's sin, that is, a position somewhere between complete guilt and blamelessness. Frederic I. Carpenter, in "Scarlet A Minus," *College English* 5 (January 1944):173, writes that "between the orthodox belief that Hester Prynne sinned utterly and the opposite romantic belief that she did not sin at all, the transcendental idealists seek to mediate." This intermediate position, very like Hawthorne's "unpardonable sin" idea, nonetheless embodies much more of an emphasis on guilt than it seems the Transcendentalists would admit.

49. Waggoner, *Hawthorne*, p. 14.

50. *Complete Works*, 5:195.

51. Ibid., p. 196.

52. Waggoner, *Hawthorne*, p. 146.

53. *Complete Works*, 3:216.

54. Ibid., p. 313.

55. Ibid., pp. 307–8.

56. F. O. Matthiessen, *American Renaissance: Art and Expression in the Age of Emerson and Whitman* (New York, 1941), p. 328.

57. *Complete Works*, 3:308.

58. Ibid.

59. Ibid., p. 200.

60. See Leo Marx, *The Machine in the Garden: Technology and the Pastoral Ideal in America* (New York, 1964) for a discussion of the influence of and the reaction to the train by writers during Hawthorne's time. For a shorter and more concentrated treatment of the influence of the train on Emerson, Thoreau, and Hawthorne, see G. Ferris Cronkhite, "The Transcendental Railroad," *New England Quarterly* 24 (September 1951):306–38.

61. *Complete Works*, 3:317.

62. Henry W. Sams, ed., *Autobiography of Brook Farm* (Englewood Cliffs, N.J., 1958), p. 6.

63. *Love Letters of Nathaniel Hawthorne, 1839–41 and 1841–63*, vol. 1 (Chicago, 1907), p. 103.

64. Arlin Turner, "Introduction," *The Blithedale Romance* (New York, 1958), p. 8.

65. *Complete Works*, 5:321.

66. Arthur Sherbo's "Albert Brisbane and Hawthorne's Holgrave and Hollingsworth," *New England Quarterly* 27 (December 1954):531–34 seems to go beyond idle speculation, however. He not only sees Brisbane as the model for these two fictional characters but makes clear their similarities as reformers and Hawthorne's attitudes toward all three as well.

67. *Complete Works*, 5:331.

68. Ibid., p. 379.

69. Ibid., p. 328.

70. Ibid., pp. 598–99.

71. Waggoner, in his chapter "The Blithedale Romance," *Hawthorne*, pp.

188–208, implicitly points to the dramaturgical imagery in the romance.

72. *Complete Works*, 5:430.

73. Ibid., p. 496.

74. Ibid., 1:220.

75. Ibid., 5:326.

76. Ibid., pp. 331–32.

77. Ibid., p. 333.

78. Ibid., pp. 342–43.

79. Ibid., p. 347.

80. Ibid., p. 361.

81. Ibid., p. 394.

82. Ibid., pp. 431–32.

83. Ibid., p. 600.

84. Lewis, *The American Adam*, pp. 122–23.

85. Hawthorne's concern about his inability to get closer to reality goes back to at least 1837. In a letter to Longfellow on July 4, cited by Randall Stewart in *American Notebooks*, p. xlii, he explains his dilemma as it concerned physical description particularly: " 'I have . . . great difficulty in the lack of materials; for I have seen so little of the world, that I have nothing but thin air to concoct my stories of, and it is not easy to give a lifelike substance to such shadowy stuff.' "

86. For a full treatment of Hawthorne's difficult last period, see Edward H. Davidson, *Hawthorne's Last Phase* (New Haven, 1949).

CONCLUSION

1. Carl Bode, "The Sound of American Literature a Century Ago," *Proceedings of the British Academy* 47 (1961):111.

2. See Harold P. Miller, "Hawthorne Surveys His Contemporaries," *American Literature* 12 (May 1940):228–35; Buford Jones, " 'The Hall of Fantasy' and the Early Hawthorne–Thoreau Relationship," *PMLA* 83 (October 1968):1429–38; and Frank Davidson, "Thoreau's Contributions to Hawthorne's *Mosses*," *New England Quarterly* 22 (December 1947):534–42.

3. Herman Melville, "Hawthorne and His Mosses," *The Literary World* (August 17, 24, 1850).

BIBLIOGRAPHY

Albion, Robert Greenhalgh. "From Sails to Spindles: Essex County in Transition." *Essex Institute Historical Collections* 95 (April 1959): 115–36.

"The American Lyceum." *Old South Leaflets*, vol. 6, no. 139, Boston: n.d. 293–305.

The American Lyceum: Its History and Contribution to Education. U.S. Department of Interior Bulletin No. 12, Washington, D.C.: Government Printing Office, 1942.

Arner, Robert D. "Hawthorne and Jones Very: Two Dimensions of Satire in 'Egotism; or, The Bosom Serpent.'" *New England Quarterly* 42 (June 1969): 267–75.

Autograph Collection. Essex Institute.

Baker, Carlos. "Emerson and Jones Very." *New England Quarterly* 7 (March 1934): 90–99.

Barber, John Warner. *Massachusetts Towns: An 1840 View.* 2nd ed., 1840; reprint ed. Barre, Mass.: Barre Publishing Company, 1963.

Bartlett, William Irving. *Jones Very: Emerson's "Brave Saint."* Durham, N.C.: Duke University Press, 1942.

Bell, Millicent. *Hawthorne's View of the Artist.* New York: State University of New York, 1962.

Berthoff, Warner B. "Jones Very: New England Mystic." *Boston Public Library Quarterly* 2 (January 1950): 63–76.

Bode, Carl. *The American Lyceum: Town Meeting of the Mind.* New York: Oxford University Press, 1956.

————. "The Sound of American Literature a Century Ago." *Proceedings of the British Academy* 47 (1961): 97–112.

Brazer, John. *Review of the Argument in Support of Natural Religion.* Cambridge, Mass.: C. Folsom, Printer to the University, 1835. Dudleian Lecture in the Essex Institute.

Brooks, Gladys. *Three Wise Virgins.* New York: E. P. Dutton & Co., Inc., 1957.

Buckham, John W. "Literary Salem." *Essex Institute Historical Collections* 63 (July 1907): 193–98.

Cameron, Kenneth Walter. *Emerson the Essayist.* 2 vols. Hartford, Conn.: Transcendental Books, 1945.

Canby, Henry Seidel. *Classic Americans: A Study of Eminent American Writers From Irving to Whitman.* New York: Harcourt, Brace & Company, 1931.

_____. *Thoreau.* Boston: Houghton Mifflin Company, 1939.

Cantwell, Robert. *Nathaniel Hawthorne: The American Years.* New York: Rinehart & Company, Inc., 1948.

Carpenter, Frederic I. "Scarlet A Minus." *College English* 5 (January 1944): 173–80.

Charvat, William. *Emerson's American Lecture Engagements: A Chronological List.* New York: The New York Public Library, 1961.

Cohen, B. Bernard. "Emerson's 'The Young American' and Hawthorne's 'The Intelligence Office.'" *American Literature* 17 (March 1954): 32–43.

Conway, Moncure D. *Life of Nathaniel Hawthorne.* London: Walter Scott, 1870.

Couser, G. Thomas. "'The Old Manse,' *Walden,* and the Hawthorne-Thoreau Relationship." *ESQ* 21 (1st Quarter 1975): 11–20.

Crews, Frederick C. *The Sins of the Fathers: Hawthorne's Psychological Themes.* New York: Oxford University Press, 1966.

Cronkhite, G. Ferris. "The Transcendental Railroad." *New England Quarterly* 24 (September 1951): 306–28.

Curti, Merle E. "John Brazer." *Dictionary of American Biography.* Vol. 2. New York: Charles Scribner's Sons, 1928–40. pp. 612–13.

Davidson, Edward H. *Hawthorne's Last Phase.* New Haven: Yale University Press, 1949.

Davidson, Frank. "Thoreau's Contributions to Hawthorne's *Mosses.*" *New England Quarterly* 20 (December 1947): 535–42.

Dennis, William D. "The Salem Charitable Mechanic Association." *Essex Institute Historical Collections* 42 (January 1906): 1–29.

Doubleday, Neal F. "Hawthorne's Criticism of New England Life." *College English* 2 (April 1941): 639–53.

_____. "Hawthorne's Satirical Allegory." *College English* 3 (January 1942): 325–37.

Elder, Marjorie J. *Nathaniel Hawthorne: Transcendental Symbolist.* Athens, Ohio: Ohio University Press, 1969.

Emerson, Ralph Waldo. *The Complete Works of Ralph Waldo Emerson.* Centenary Edition. Edited by Edward Waldo Emerson. 12 vols. Boston and New York: Houghton, Mifflin Company, 1903–1904.

————. *The Correspondence of Emerson and Carlyle.* Edited by Joseph Slater. New York: Columbia University Press, 1964.

————. *The Early Lectures of Ralph Waldo Emerson.* Edited by Stephen E. Whicher and Robert E. Spiller. 2 vols. Cambridge, Mass.: Harvard University Press, 1959.

————. *The Journals and Miscellaneous Notebooks of Ralph Waldo Emerson.* Edited by William H. Gilman et al. 8 vols. Cambridge, Mass.: Belknap Press of Harvard University Press, 1960–70.

————. *Journals of Ralph Waldo Emerson.* Edited by Edward Waldo Emerson and Waldo Emerson Forbes. 10 vols. Boston and New York: Houghton Mifflin Company, 1909–1914.

————. *The Letters of Ralph Waldo Emerson.* Edited by Ralph L. Rusk. 6 vols. New York: Columbia University Press, 1939.

————. "New Poetry." *The Dial: A Magazine for Literature, Philosophy, and Religion.* Vol. 1. New York: Russell & Russell, Inc., 1961, pp. 220–32.

Erskine, John. "Hawthorne." *The Cambridge History of American Literature.* Edited by William P. Trent et al. Vol. 2. New York: The Macmillan Company, 1918, pp. 16–31.

Faust, Bertha. *Hawthorne's Contemporaneous Reputation: A Study of Literary Opinion in America and England. 1828–1864.* 1939; reprint ed. New York: Octagon Books, Inc., 1968.

Felt, Joseph B. *Annals of Salem.* Vol. 2. Salem: W. & S. B. Ives; Boston: James Munroe & Co., 1849.

Flanagan, John T. "Emerson as a Critic of Fiction," *Philological Quarterly* 15 (January 1936): 30–45.

Frothingham, Octavius B. *Recollections and Impressions: 1822–1890.* New York: G. P. Putnam's Sons, 1891.

————. *Theodore Parker: A Biography.* Boston: J. R. Osgood & Company, 1874.

————. *Transcendentalism in New England: A History.* 1876; reprint ed. New York: Harper & Brothers, 1959.

Gittleman, Edwin. *Jones Very: The Effective Years: 1833–1840.* New York: Columbia University Press, 1967.

Gray, Henry David. *Emerson: A Statement of New England Transcendentalism as Expressed in the Philosophy of Its Chief Exponent.* 1917; reprint ed. New York: Frederick Ungar Publishing Co., 1965.

Hall, Lawrence S. *Hawthorne: Critic of Society.* New Haven: Yale University Press, 1944.

Harding, Walter. *The Days of Henry Thoreau.* New York: Alfred A. Knopf, 1966.

Hawthorne, Julian. *Nathaniel Hawthorne and His Wife: A Biography.* 2 vols. Boston: James R. Osgood and Company, 1885.

Hawthorne, Nathaniel. *The Complete Works of Nathaniel Hawthorne, with Introductory Notes.* Riverside Edition. Edited by George P. Lathrop. 12 vols. Boston: Houghton, Mifflin and Company, 1883.

_____. *The American Notebooks.* Edited by Randall Stewart. New Haven: Yale University Press, 1932.

Hochfield, George, ed. *Selected Writings of the American Transcendentalists.* New York: The New American Library, 1966.

Hoeltje, Hubert H. *Inward Sky: The Mind and Heart of Nathaniel Hawthorne.* Durham, N.C.: Duke University Press, 1962.

_____. "The Writing of *The Scarlet Letter.*" *New England Quarterly* 27 (September 1954): 326–46.

Hutchison, William R. *The Transcendentalist Ministers: Church Reform in the New England Renaissance.* New Haven: Yale University Press, 1959.

Jones, Buford. "'The Hall of Fantasy' and the Early Hawthorne-Thoreau Relationship." *PMLA* 83 (October 1968): 1429–38.

Lamson, Asa. Unpublished 1860 Almanac Diary. Essex Institute Diary Collection.

Lathrop, Rose Hawthorne. *Memories of Hawthorne.* London: Kegan Paul, Trench, Trubner & Co., 1897.

Lewis, R. W. B. *The American Adam: Innocence, Tragedy, and Tradition in the Nineteenth Century.* Chicago: University of Chicago Press, 1955.

Loggins, Vernon. *The Hawthornes.* New York: Columbia University Press, 1951.

Love Letters of Nathaniel Hawthorne, 1839–41 and 1841–63. 2 vols. Privately printed. Chicago: The Society of the Dofobs, 1907.

Lyons, Nathan, ed. *Jones Very: Selected Poems.* New Brunswick, N.J.: Rutgers University Press, 1966.

Samuel McIntire Issue. *Essex Institute Historical Collections* 93 (April–July 1957).

Male, Roy R. *Hawthorne's Tragic Vision.* Austin, Tex.: University of Texas Press, 1957.

Martin, Terence. *Nathaniel Hawthorne.* New York: Twayne Publishers, Inc., 1965.

Marx, Leo. *The Machine in the Garden: Technology and the Pastoral Ideal in America*. New York: Oxford University Press, 1964.

Matthiessen, F. O. *American Renaissance: Art and Expression in the Age of Emerson and Whitman*. New York: Oxford University Press, 1941.

Mead, David. *Yankee Eloquence in the Middle West: The Ohio Lyceum, 1850–1870*. East Lansing, Mich.: Michigan State College Press, 1951.

Melville, Herman. "Hawthorne and His Mosses." *The Literary World*, August 17, 24, 1850.

Miller, Harold P. "Hawthorne Surveys His Contemporaries." *American Literature* 12 (May 1940): 228–35.

Morison, Samuel Eliot. *The Maritime History of Massachusetts, 1783–1860*. Boston: Houghton Mifflin Company, 1921.

Mozart Association. *Constitution of the Mozart Association, Instituted in Salem, June, 1825*. Salem: printed by Warwick Palfray, June, 1826.

Nichols, Jonathan P., Jr. "Lecture Delivered Before the Society of O. A." Unpublished manuscript. Gilbert Streeter Collection. Essex Institute.

Oliver, Henry K. *Historical Sketch of the Salem Lyceum with a list of the Officers and Lectures Since its formation in 1830 and an extract from the address of Gen. Henry K. Oliver delivered at the Opening of the Fiftieth Annual Course of Lectures*, Nov. 13, 1878. Salem: Press of the Salem Gazette, 1879.

Osgood, Charles, and Batchelder, H. M. "Salem." *Standard History of Essex County, Massachusetts*. Comp. by Cyrus Mason Tracy, William E. Graves, and Henry M. Batchelder. Boston: C. F. Jewett & Co., 1878.

Parker, Theodore. *Theodore Parker: An Anthology*. Edited by Henry Steele Commager. Boston: Beacon Press, 1960.

Peabody Letters. Essex Institute Autograph Collection.

Perry, Bliss. "The Centenary of Hawthorne." *Atlantic* 94 (August 1904): 195–206.

Pickman, Mary. Unpublished Diary. Essex Institute Diary Collection.

Pollard, John A. "Lyceum Lectures Drew Brilliant Minds to Salem." *Salem Evening News*, December 12, 1929.

"The Rage for Lectures." The Salem *Gazette*, March 14, 1943.

Rantoul, Robert Samuel. "Story of Old Lyceum Hall." *Salem Evening News*, March 5, 1915.

Rosa, Alfred F., ed. " 'Aesthetic Culture': A Lyceum Lecture by William Silsbee." *Essex Institute Historical Collections* 107 (January 1971): 35–61.

————. "Alcott and Montessori." *Connecticut Review* 3 (October 1969): 98–103.

Rusk, Ralph L. *The Life of Ralph Waldo Emerson.* New York: Charles Scribner's Sons, 1949.

The Salem *Gazette*, 1825–60.

Salem Lyceum Collection, with Treasurers' Reports (1832–98) and Other Memorabilia. Essex Institute.

Salem Lyceum Minutes. Essex Institute.

The Salem *Observer*, 1830–59.

The Salem *Register*, 1841–76.

Sams, Henry W., ed. *The Autobiography of Brook Farm.* Englewood Cliffs, N.J.: Prentice-Hall, Inc., 1958.

Sealts, Merton M., and Ferguson, Alfred R., eds. *Emerson's 'Nature'—Origin, Growth, Meaning.* New York: Dodd, Mead & Company, Inc., 1969.

Shanley, J. Lyndon. *The Making of Walden, with the Text of the First Version.* Chicago: University of Chicago Press, 1957.

Sharf, Frederic Alan. "Charles Osgood: The Life and Times of a Salem Portrait Painter." *Essex Institute Historical Collections* 102 (July 1966): 203–12.

Shepard, Odell. *Pedlar's Progress: The Life of Bronson Alcott.* Boston: Little, Brown and Company, 1937.

Sherbo, Arthur. "Albert Brisbane and Hawthorne's Holgrave and Hollingsworth." *New England Quarterly* 27 (December 1954): 531–34.

Sherman, Stuart P. *Americans.* New York: Charles Scribner's Sons, 1922.

Stearns, Frank P. *The Life and Genius of Nathaniel Hawthorne.* Philadelphia: J. B. Lippincott Company, 1906.

Stern, Milton R. "American Values and Romantic Fiction." *American Fiction: Historical and Critical Essays.* Edited by James Nagel. Boston: Northeastern University Press, 1977, pp. 13–33.

Stewart, Randall. "Charles W. Upham." *Dictionary of American Biography.* Vol. 19. New York: Charles Scribner's Sons, 1928–40, pp. 121–22.

————. "Hawthorne and Politics: Unpublished Letters to William B. Pike." *New England Quarterly* 5 (April 1932): 237–63.

————. *Nathaniel Hawthorne: A Biography.* New Haven: Yale University Press, 1948.

Stovall, Floyd. *American Idealism.* 1943; reissued Port Washington, N.Y.: Kennikat Press, 1965.

Tapley, Harriet Silvester. *Salem Imprints: 1768–1825.* Salem: Essex Institute, 1927.

Tharp, Louise Hall. *The Peabody Sisters of Salem.* Boston: Little, Brown and Company, 1950.

Thoreau, Henry David. *The Correspondence of Henry David Thoreau.* Edited by Walter Harding and Carl Bode. New York: New York University Press, 1958.

Turner, Arlin. "Hawthorne and Reform." *New England Quarterly* 15 (December 1942): 700–714.

————. "Introduction." *The Blithedale Romance.* New York: W. W. Norton & Co., Inc., 1958.

Upham, Charles W. "A Circular Letter Issued Pursuant to the Vote of a Convention Held at Topsfield, Dec. 30, 1829, for Establishing a County Lyceum." *Essex Institute Historical Collections* 18 (December 1881): 293–306.

Van Doren, Mark. *Nathaniel Hawthorne.* New York: William Sloane Associates, 1949.

Waggoner, Hyatt Howe. *Hawthorne: A Critical Study.* Rev. ed. Cambridge, Mass.: Belknap Press of Harvard University Press, 1963.

Warren, Austin, ed. *Nathaniel Hawthorne: Representative Selections.* New York: American Book Company, 1934.

Waters, Susan Louise. Unpublished Diary. Essex Institute Diary Collection.

Wichelns, Herbert A. "Ralph Waldo Emerson." *A History and Criticism of American Public Address.* Edited by William Norwood Brigance. Vol. 2. New York: McGraw-Hill Book Company, 1943, pp. 501–25.

Winters, Yvor. *Maule's Curse.* Norfolk, Conn.: New Directions, 1938.

Index